the mom Babes

A Motherhood Anthology. ♥

CHRISTINA WALSH
CAROLYN TURKINGTON

TSPA The Self Publishing Agency Inc.

Christina Walsh, Carolyn Turkington

The MomBabes

TSPA The Self Publishing Agency Inc.

First Edition

Softcover ISBN 978-1-7776014-1-6
Hardcover ISBN 978-1-7776014-0-9
eBook ISBN 978-1-7776014-2-3

Cover & Book Design | Kristy Hill

Editor | Tara McGuire

Publishing Support | TSPA The Self Publishing Agency Inc.

♥

To our MomBabe Community

Thank you for always showing up for us. You allow
us to watch our dream come to life, everyday.
We're always rooting for you.

Table of Contents

♥

Forward

Welcome, MomBabe.

Welcome to the coolest non-member club since The Pink Ladies, we're so happy you're here. We know that being a new mom is hard. Being a seasoned mom is hard. Being a working mom is hard. Let's just say being a mom is hard. But what if it didn't have to feel hard or lonely or scary? What if we could help you feel a little more loved, a little more encouraged, maybe even inspired in your daily mom life?

We've built a community of MomBabes where we scratch off the "World's Best Mom" title and "feel" satisfied with who we are. Hands up for "World's Okayest Mom!" Good enough is often all that's necessary, and being able to share other's stories of the highs and lows, the messy, the humdrum, the beautiful, can make us feel more well, normal.

It all started with a cup of coffee. Well, actually a box of coffee. Like wine, the box is cool.

As a second time mom, I knew how important it was for me to establish mom friends. My sister Carolyn and I had always imagined we would have children but never imagined we would be on maternity leave at the same time. With a five year gap between my first and second it felt a little like being a "new mom" all over, except I knew from experience that one day *I would sleep again.*

Chatting with some fellow mamas during a "Mommy and Me" sing along, I just wanted to hug them all and say, *I promise you're doing a f*cking rad job.* I also wanted to be able to connect with the women on more than just the surface level at circle time. There I was sitting cross legged, clapping my hands, trying to sing, "The wheels on the bus go round and round...how are you?... let's hang out!..." I wanted to find the kind of moms I could have a running group text with, a network I could message twenty-four hours a day because I knew someone would most likely be awake. I was longing for deeper conversation about more than just my kid's names and what snacks they like. The answer is Piper and Quinn, and goldfish crackers, by the way. Sure, my kids are great, *but I'm great too*. So, I did something totally crazy. Outrageous really. I was a wild woman. I invited them over. All of them. I posted my address on the bulletin board at the community center with a note that said, *I'll be here with coffee and donuts. If you need a friend, come over.*

All weekend I wondered if anyone would show up. Tuesday morning, I kinda tidied my kitchen and hit the drive-thru for a box of coffee, and donuts. Then a crazy thing happened. Right on time, a parade of cars rolled down my street and stopped. Thirteen moms with babes and diaper bags in hand, walked in one after the other…and I knew right then, we all needed each other.

Remember the best first date you ever had? That morning was the closest I'd been to a first date in over ten years, and I wondered how to ask these women on a second date. *What do I do? Do I text? How long do I wait?* I was sweating through my all natural deodorant thinking about it. A little self doubt set in. *Did they have fun? Did they like me? Did they like each other?* I had to keep reapplying my natural deodorant.

The next week, I channelled some Brene Brown, gave myself the "be brave," pep talk and hit the drive-thru once again. Not only did the "regulars" show up, they invited their friends. When moms I'd never met before started knocking on my door and stepping out of their comfort zones, just like I did, I was so proud. YES! You go, Mama! And this time my sister Carolyn and her three month old son, Reece came too. We looked at each other and we had all the feels. This was special.

Those early weeks and months after a baby arrives pull you into a world you never quite step out of again. Becoming a parent is like stepping into Narnia; once you've walked through that wardrobe you're changed, even if you do eventually find your way back out.

Coffee Club as we called it then, was a simple idea but what has evolved from it are rich and meaningful relationships that are not simple at all. Meeting every week to be ourselves first and share our mom musings is something that fills us all up. The epiphany for Carolyn and me, as we watched all of our new friends share their stories and chat together over coffee was this...moms need other moms. Women need other women.

We realized The MomBabes was more than just a bunch of women in my living room. This could be a meaningful movement for ALL MOMS looking for something more genuine and real.

This is how the MomBabes community began, but why did we need it? How did we know we had to be brave? How did we know that one's community can literally make the difference between struggling and surviving?

Three months earlier we had a near death experience. We didn't die, our Dad did, and we were near. When you hold the hand of a dying person, you are hand in hand with death. You feel it. The wave comes over you, and it tugs you, but you know you're strong enough to let go while you guide your loved one to the other side. We were wrapped in grief and welcoming babies into the world at the same time.

We don't often consider grief and loss as part of the process of entering motherhood. The enormous responsibility of parenting can hit hard and some-times we're left aching for our former lives. Kinda like our old self died. Nobody talks at the gender reveal parties or baby showers about the sense of loss that can come with having a child. It's always a celebration but we rarely discuss the, "I'll never be the same again," realization.

Parental grief can also rise when you send that child to kindergarten, to college, or become empty nesters. Maybe it's after a separation of friendship, or divorce, losing your job, or trying to restart your career after being home raising babies. The losses we have felt in 2020 alone feel suffocating.

Many moms don't acknowledge the full spectrum of their feelings. Especially the less attractive ones. Loss and grief, fear, guilt and shame, even anger. We know, moms feel all the feels, but we also know that one of the best ways to heal is by sharing in a safe community, if we are brave enough to reach out to one.

Carolyn and I stood in a room of 300 people at our dad's funeral and saw a whole life gathered together, his community, our community. It was a pretty incredible gift. We held hands reading our Dad's eulogy. We closed our eyes at the end, embracing those warm tears and whispered, "Don't forget, don't ever forget this moment." Our father's legacy filled the room and in that moment we realized how much of his legacy was us.

Our babies were five years, five months, and five weeks old at our dad's funeral. A few months later, once the fog had lifted, we felt pulled to something more. While it's hard to imagine there could be a silver lining in losing our father, the idea of legacy swirled around in our heads. What would our legacy be?

We decided not to wait until the end of our lifespans to discover our purpose. Let's start thinking about legacy now. Grief became our greatest teacher — *what if every day was a celebration of life?*

Carolyn and I didn't dream of being authors. We didn't walk around with pens and paper in our hands, or have boxes filled with old journals. We didn't get A's in English or even major in English in university. Writing a book was not on our bucket list. However, we have been told countless times that we have enough stories to fill a book. Doesn't everyone?

We didn't get caught up in the how, the why was a bigger question. We started with what we knew. We took our living room full of moms to the internet so more people could join the party. We showed up every day just being ourselves, reminding moms they are enough, their bodies are enough, their efforts are enough, and their dreams are worth it. Let's not wait for the right time. Put on your bathing suit when you're not a size six, make time for you, set those goals. Don't stop DREAMING!!

So, along with that box of coffee, we're going to toss you up some truth salad. We are better together. We are better when everyone shares their truth. Everyone has a story. Big, little, revolutionary, transformational, inspiring, funny. This book is a big bowl of salad. There is something in it for everyone. Pick out what you love and serve it up.

The MomBabes started with two women, which became fifteen, and has turned into more than we could ever have imagined. And now here we are with twenty authors, moms who have each written a piece of their heart on paper. We are so proud to be sharing these pages with you and with them, because they are the true stars.

Is there any better time to build a solid community than right now? Trust us on this one — you want to be a MomBabe! We promise to support and encourage you with real talk where we shoot straight from our love handles while keeping our wine (we mean coffee) cups full and our dishwasher empty. May your coffee be hot and your scrunchie game strong.

Christina
♥ +
Carolyn

Gillian

♥

Why Didn't Anyone Tell Me?

I didn't know that during childbirth there was a very good chance I would poop on the table.

I also didn't know that it would feel like the baby was coming out of my rear end.

To be fair, there is a lot of pressure down there. A watermelon being pushed out of a lemon-sized hole type of pressure. And with that pressure comes a very good chance that whatever else is inside, will also come out.

So yes, you will likely poop on the table.

In front of people.

I was mortified. The nurse tried to tell me everyone does it, but at that point I figured she was just humouring me, trying to soothe the shame of having just defecated for an audience of strangers.

And oh, the butt pain. Thirty hours into a thirty-one-hour labour with our first born, and you know that feeling when you land tailbone first on the crossbar of a bike? That's what I was feeling, except it went on forever.

I stopped. The pushing, the groaning, the encouragement from my sweet, but totally helpless in the moment, husband. Full stop. I yelled, "Wait a minute!" The doctor and nurse looked up from between my legs, not sure what was wrong.

"Would somebody please do something about my ASS?"

The doctor gasped. The nurse definitely snorted. They quickly recovered and provided some freezing to the area in question.

But WHY didn't anyone tell me this was a thing? Why didn't my mom, or my friends that had gone before me, SAY something? I honestly thought something was wrong with my rear end.

I went to the childbirth class. Okay, I skipped the eight-week session, because who has time for eight weeks of how to hold a plastic baby? In hindsight it might have been worth it. Ignorant first-time parents, we defiantly stuck with our one-day slackers' class. We heard the stories, watched the videos, and learned how to hold the plastic baby.

But never did the instructor mention back labour, or table poop.

I definitely would have remembered table poop.

I didn't know that breastfeeding can hurt. That it doesn't always work. That I would feed and feed, and lose all that effort with one tube-shaped spit-up. That it is possible to hold my baby without both of us crying.

Nobody said anything about postpartum anxiety. About how the fear of being away from my baby would grip me to my core. I didn't know why I was feeling completely irrational, and unable to control it.

Not one person mentioned that my libido might disappear. That it's normal to lose all desire for the first few months, or even years after childbirth. To feel so tired that I couldn't possibly imagine ever feeling sexy again. To feel huge guilt for not wanting to get intimate.

No one told me that losing my temper doesn't make me a bad mom. That losing my shit, sobbing in the kitchen, does not make me a bad mom. That it's okay to need a break.

I didn't know that having a kid with a combo-platter diagnosis of autism, ADHD, anxiety, and Developmental Coordination Disorder, would make me feel lost every single day. That I would feel helpless. That I would experience emotional exhaustion like I never knew was possible. That I would resent having to work so hard.

I have spent much of the last thirteen years believing that I am the only one who feels these things. That I am the only one who has these thoughts. That I am the only one.

That something is wrong with me.

Despite the talk of villages, despite the mom groups, despite the coffee chats, motherhood can be exceptionally lonely. I felt alone in my thoughts, unable to share, terrified that I was the only one who felt this way.

Because we don't *talk* about this stuff. We don't admit that we're feeling the feelings, and thinking the thoughts. None of my mom friends have ever shared that they lost interest in sex. None of them have ever told me they are suffering with hemorrhoids. Not one of them has admitted to not liking their kid every now and then. None of them have admitted to feeling like a bad mom.

What we see 98% of the time is the highlight reel. Very few people share the back story, the hard stuff, the less-than-stellar moments. I get it, we don't want to invite everyone in, we don't want to face rejection from what might be an unwelcome or awkward conversation, we don't want to make a big deal about it.

But here's the thing: If almost no one shares the real stuff, how do we know what's actually normal? How do we know others are experiencing the same thing? Barely anyone is sharing the failures, the mistakes, or the struggles.

What we see on social media is the shiny, picture-perfect, glossed-over reality. The white kitchens with pristine Carrara marble countertops. The matching outfits where every family member is facing the camera with sparkly holiday smiles.

Yes, even the dog.

It's so easy to play the comparison game. And if we go down the scroll hole and follow all the influencers whose jobs are to showcase carefully curated beauty and perfection, then OF COURSE we will feel less than. If we never see our real experiences mirrored back to us, if no one is being completely open and acknowledging the truths of how hard life can be sometimes, then how can we ever know that what we're experiencing is common, appropriate, and totally okay? That there is NO reason to feel embarrassed or ashamed.

There are moments I feel like a good mom. Hell, even a super mom. Those magical moments where I try a new tactic to get my kid to follow instructions, and IT WORKS. He emerges from his smelly early-teen vortex of a room without an argument. I am a FREAKING PARENTING GENIUS!

But I also feel like a shitty mom on a daily basis. I yell. I lose my patience. I give myself time-outs because I don't want to be in the same room as my kid. I regret how I handle situations. I say things I am convinced will be the comment they will tell their therapist in twenty years.

We have so much more information now than the generations before us, more knowledge about behaviours, mental health diagnoses, about social skills, and appropriate stages of development. But there are also SO many more perceived rules now about how we "should" be parenting. Now every parenting expert and article has more ways to show us how we are screwing up our kids.

"Oh, I always speak softly to my child. I'm always patient." This is amazing advice, Sheila, but in all honesty it makes me feel like shit. When you have a hormonal thirteen year old kid on the autism spectrum, navigating ADHD with a side helping of anxiety, SOFTLY DOESN'T ALWAYS WORK. When you've been listening to him making siren sounds for three solid hours and then have the audacity to gently request he feed the cats, "patient" only lasts so long.

It doesn't actually matter what Sheila says. Sheila has her own stuff to deal with, and she is likely not talking about it because she feels embarrassed and thinks something is wrong with her.

Spoiler: There is nothing wrong with Sheila.

There is nothing wrong with any of us.

I have two kids I adore. I have two kids I am obsessed with (to be clear, I only have two kids, there's no third kid that I am not obsessed with) and those two kids have a mom who is trying her freaking hardest, every single day.

We are human, and we are raising humans. Becoming a mom did not magically erase our own anxieties, delete our own goals and desires, take away our stress responses, insert endless patience, or install the "mom knowledge" microchip that lets us know exactly what to say or how to react in every moment. We make mistakes.

There is no reason to be embarrassed. There is no reason to feel ashamed.

Except for maybe that one time I pooped on a table.

———

Gillian lives by the mantra, "Done is better than perfect," which comes in handy when your superpower is avoiding housework. Gillian is the founder of Mom Camp and the host of Mom Camp: Around the Campfire Podcast empowering moms to put themselves back on their own priority list and re-ignite their sparks. She dreams of travelling to NYC, with unlimited Broadway tickets.

Gillian Behnke

momcamplife.com
🄾 momcamplife

Meredith

♥

Babysteps to Motherhood

I wasn't the girl who dreamed of her fairytale wedding. No, not at all, but I did have dreams of being a mother. I had sought every opportunity to be with children since I could remember. I had excitedly picked out a daughter's name, Claudia, after reading the Babysitters Club books. But at fifteen years old I was diagnosed with a fertility syndrome and was told it was a leading infertility condition among women. For me this diagnosis penetrated my entire being. I felt a loss of my dream even as premature as it was at that age.

After living many years with the syndrome and the constant reminder of my hormone imbalance as another month passed without a normal cycle, I decided to seek further medical attention and see a fertility doctor who could assess my condition. Up until that point, to protect myself from the fear of not being able to have children and disappointing a partner, I had shied away from serious relationships or picked partners who I was assured didn't have expectations of having a family. Even at the time of my initial diagnosis, I was innately aware of the role women play in childbearing and the fact that I could be considered faulty merchandise if I wasn't able to produce children for someone who wanted them.

After confirming my worst nightmare, that I indeed still had the syndrome, the doctor's parting words as I left the office, "Don't wait too long to start trying," rang in my head. I wondered if I would ever have the chance to become a mother.

Single and approaching my 36th birthday I shed many tears. For the first time in my life, I felt completely rudderless and everything seemed upside down. My mother, in an attempt to lift my spirits, suggested I go away, as travel had brought me so much pleasure in my twenties and thirties. So I did just that and planned a week-long trip. That's when I met George.

The moment I met George while travelling in Havana, I just knew he was someone I had to continue to get to know. Because we met on the second to last day before I was to return home, our relationship developed very innocently by phone and email over months and months. For the first time in my life, I decided to be open and vulnerable which allowed me to completely trust myself. My heart would skip a thousand beats when I heard a text from him, as it was our chance to continue to exchange words, ideas and share our dreams.

George knew every bit of me that I had hidden from the rest of the world, and he accepted me and whatever our future would be. The way he looked at me when we were together let me know that he supported all my dreams. He had a great love of children, a father of one himself, Claudia. Learning that his daughter's name was the same I had chosen for mine was a sign of good things to come.

George and I committed to each other when I returned to Havana four months after our initial meeting. I attempted to travel to Cuba every two to three months as this was much easier than the long process to acquire a visitor visa for him to visit me. After visiting George six months later, even before I left to return home, I felt ill. I was beginning to wonder if I was pregnant, but too scared to even think of that possibility in case it wasn't true. Maybe I had just picked up a virus while travelling? Back home while attending a conference I decided to bolt out on my lunch hour and get a blood test and quickly return hoping no one would notice my absence. Shock flooded through me when I answered my phone the next day. I stood motionless, speechless, staring up at an enormous globe hanging from the ceiling in the conference centre. I was pregnant! I thanked the universe for picking me to be this child's mother.

The nine months of pregnancy that followed were challenging for many reasons. I traveled to see George three times while I was pregnant, which was a feat as I struggled with severe morning sickness every day until the birth of our baby. Each time George and I were reunited I arrived with my belly that much bigger. When we were together my sickness seemed to lift a little; I bathed in the attention and touch of my partner and enjoyed the days I didn't have to be strong. When I left Cuba that last time, it was hard to deny how scared I was that George and I may be faced with our longest separation and the possibility that he may not be able to attend the birth of our child, Mariah. Since we weren't together during the pregnancy we had named our baby girl so that we could find peace in referring to her by name and starting our bonding with our unborn child, in our own special way.

We had fulfilled all the listed requirements for George's visitor visa twice and been rejected. We decided to apply a third time which would be the last chance for George to be present at Mariah's birth. When I saw my phone ring I knew it was the important news we had been waiting for. Hands freezing cold in fear, I picked up the phone. Our final request for a visitor visa had been denied once again. I crumbled. Seven-and-a-half months pregnant, with tears in my eyes, there wasn't anyone else in the world I wanted beside me for the birth of our first child.

Fortunately my mom was visiting from across the country and she consoled me the best way she could. And like many bad days, after a good rest, I started the next day to find solutions, peace inside, and focus on what was in my control. I didn't shed another tear after that night. There was no time to feel sorry for myself, after all, having a child was the honour I had been waiting for since I was a child myself.

Our baby girl was born two weeks earlier than her due date. George was present on the phone during the first part of my labour, as he has been for all the other medical appointments. The medical team who supported me had been briefed on our situation and somehow they all found exactly the right words to comfort me. One nurse commented that the experience was special because she had never been able to give 100% of her attention to the birthing mother.

Though both of my parents had offered to be there for me something inside told me I wanted to experience my child's birth by myself. As the hours ticked by and a day passed, it seemed that everything was progressing well medically, but somehow my mind and body were at odds. The baby and myself were healthy by all accounts, heartbeat, blood pressure, so what was going on? I remember my doula asking me to address any blockages I had mentally. She knew. Although I had shown strength and flexibility, this was still not what I had planned or envisioned for our family and deep in my core I may not have fully accepted it. I broke down crying.

Mariah was born less than an hour after that, on the same day as her sister Claudia's birthday. This time the tears that flowed were happy ones.

———

Every night, without fail Meredith unwinds with a hot bath, maybe that's why she's rarely awake after 10 p.m. She dislikes negativity of any sort. Is that ironic? Possibly. Meredith loves her corporate work life and travelling. Her favourite destination is Cuba to spend time with family, including her bonus daughter, and to expose her two children to the culture and language.

Meredith Luksha
🄾 meredithluksha

Shilo

♥

Keeping My Secret

I found out I was pregnant just before I turned eighteen. That left me feeling troubled. I was worried about my future and what people would say, especially my parents. I knew they wouldn't approve of my pregnancy or who I became pregnant by. I thought about abortion but I panicked and let fear take over. I decided I would keep it a secret and hoped to miscarry. Maybe nature would make the decision for me. I never went to see a doctor or asked for support from anyone. The fewer people who knew, the better. My secret was safe.

I took a mixture of over the counter pills. Never too many to overdose but enough that maybe something would happen and I would never have to tell my secret. I starved myself. If I didn't eat then maybe the baby wouldn't develop. However, I began to feel the baby growing. I would push my stomach against the counter corners until it hurt thinking this would cause a miscarriage. I was afraid of what I was doing and what was to come. I tried superstitious things like rubbing a penny for luck, wishing on stars and praying to God to do the right thing. I would whisper, "Keep this baby safe." Every day the guilt swallowed me up. I felt desperate and alone all the while carrying a child inside me.

I had awful morning sickness and would hide upstairs until it subsided enough to come down and try to behave like a regular teenager. I'd wear baggy clothes and suck in my belly as best as I could.

Eventually this all became too much for me to carry alone. I was still living with my parents but I wasn't going to be able to deliver a baby in my bedroom, so I told my best friend and one of my sisters. I set a plan to move out of town and have the baby with a midwife. I figured no hospital, no paperwork, and my secret would still be safe. I would give the baby up for adoption and move back home like nothing had changed.

At thirty-seven weeks I went to see a doctor at a walk-in clinic. They were surprised how far along I was with zero medical attention. I was sent for my first sonogram. Those photos sat on my nightstand and I planned to keep them forever because soon it would be all I had left. I found out the baby was breech so my plan for a home delivery wasn't possible and I was scheduled for a cesarean birth. I was petrified. I had worked so hard to hide all this.

I was admitted to the hospital the night before my surgery. The staff spent time with me discussing my decision about adoption. They talked about foster care and what that option was like. It was then I decided foster care was a better choice until I was ready to tell my secret. My best friend kept her word and held my hand through it all, keeping my pregnancy confidential. I wasn't alone. She stayed with me that night at the hospital, two eighteen-year-olds having the most unusual sleepover. And the next morning my baby girl was born.

The epidural didn't work so I was sedated during delivery, when I woke up a man from social services came into my room. He began asking questions about my baby. I remember feeling uncertain. I was still quite groggy from the anesthetic and had to ask my friend for the answers. Aware of my state of mind he said he would be back in a couple days to follow up regarding foster care. I couldn't believe all that was happening!

That evening I was more alert and I wanted to see my daughter. When the nurse brought her in I could not have imagined a more beautiful creation. Time seemed to stand still as I stared in awe. Her hair was dark brown and her skin appeared darker than my own. She was so tiny and peaceful. I had a restrained desire of feeling the emotions a mother should have looking at her newborn. She wasn't going home with me but I was her mom, and my secret was now in the world.

For the first time in nine months I felt happiness and yet I was fearful because I knew I would have to give her back. How could a teen mom be successful? I didn't see how I could raise a child and earn a degree on my own. I wanted a career and stability, I didn't want to be a stereotype. An overwhelming feeling took over but I knew I had to tell my family. I had to be brave for my daughter. She deserved it.

I'm close to my grandmother on my mom's side so I called and told her. Most people would break the news by announcing, "I'm pregnant," but I had to skip that part and said "I've had a baby," and next told her my plan. She wept. She was now a great-grandmother. Without hesitation she offered me love and support and told me I would still be a successful young woman, like I always imagined. She would help me. The weight began to lift, maybe my parents' reaction would be like this too.

Could I do this?

My grandmother called my parents and told them what I'd been through and that I was now a mother. I felt a lump in my throat when my mom called. I dreaded her disappointment but even more so, I feared her abandoning me. She spoke quietly and softly with many long pauses. She was worried about me but also disappointed I hadn't told them. Their first grandchild and my neurotic fear kept us from sharing the experience together. I had guilt for denying them of this.

The next day as I anxiously waited for my family to come and meet our newest member, I felt awkward but at the same time I had joy and wonder inside me. My sisters were overjoyed to be aunties. My parents were happy and their eyes sparkled when they held their granddaughter for the first time. My mom gave me a long hug. A hug that held the emotions of a mother's love, support, comfort and concern. My fear and anxiety began to fade and it was then I felt ready to be a mom.

I was grateful for those who were there for me. I always had the support but was too afraid to reach out. I lived in fear instead of doing what felt right. The moment I told my family about my daughter I no longer felt alone and knew we could enjoy beginning our lives together.

The little girl who was once a secret is now a caring and aspiring young adult. I raised my daughter Kiara myself, with the love and support of my family by my side. When I struggled they reminded me I didn't have to do it alone.

With her as my motivation, I completed college and I work each day to better myself. I now have two beautiful daughters who encourage me to be a role model for them, although they probably teach me more about life than I teach them. I've learned that life is unpredictable. That acceptance is powerful, it can be hard but also enlightening, and that I do not have to be alone.

When Kiara was six years old she surprised me by saying, "Life is a story. We write our own stories," and she's right! I couldn't be happier that I chose to keep and raise my secret as a part of my life's story.

Shilo loves her work in direct patient care at a large doctors office. It irritates her when things are not returned to their proper places...agreed! Shilo's go-to for self care is an aroma scented bath or a latte. Lazy Sundays you'll find this dedicated mom of two cozied up on the couch with a blanket and her homemade fresh-baked goodies. Her favourite book is this one.

Shilo Koide

🅕 Shilo Koide

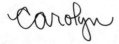

Pep Talk:
Change of Plans

Sometimes life is all about how you handle plan B.

A very smart mom told me once, "I think it's a good idea to have a motherhood preference, rather than a set motherhood plan." #nailedit.

There is nothing more reassuring than a colour coded agenda, a to-list and a Pinterest-ready pantry but sometimes you have to put down the highlighter and look at your own highlight REAL. The mess is okay because you live there.

We can plan for the natural childbirth, to be queen of the snacks, to arrive ten minutes early, and fingers crossed to not lose socks in the dryer, but my kid *literally* is the kid who always has mismatched socks.

Let's be honest, we can't curate motherhood. Motherhood is not perfect and neither are we.

Carolyn

Natasha

♥

Lost and Found

I never imagined life with children. I wanted a career. I was a cop. I had a work family and that was enough for me.

I worked patrol, a forty-eight-hour rotating schedule. I loved it. It was fast-paced, high adrenaline and high pressure.

I loved the flexibility to take off to Mexico on a last minute red-eye flight because of my schedule. My downtime could be on the beach with a piña colada, and I was definitely not sitting by the kiddie pool. I had made my choice, I worked hard for my career, and it was my identity.

Then…came the love of my life. As soon as I saw him, the words, "His wife makes his lunch," popped into my head. I had already sworn off dating anyone in my industry and I sure as hell wasn't making anyone a lunch. It took a chance encounter and then a solid friendship built on many tests of trust before I took a leap of faith. My life took a 180 degree turn. I was in love with the most supportive, kind man and together we had the same dream of travelling to Scotland, fighting crime, getting married, having kids, and a twelve-foot Christmas tree. Together we could have it all.

I never considered the impact motherhood would have on my career. I didn't realize this one tiny human (that I had to keep alive) would be the hardest job I would ever have. Oh, and the most thankless and underpaid.

I was a skilled, trained, experienced cop. I showed up every day prepared and ready to take on anything from traffic complaints to the worst human the world has ever seen. I could be at a shoplifting call only to be suddenly driving with my lights and sirens to a robbery in progress. My job was to show up, fix the problem, and save people. How could one tiny human make me feel so helpless?

My whole birth experience went nothing like planned. My body let me down, it failed me. After twelve hours of labour, a catheter put in incorrectly that I could feel, and an epidural that didn't work due to an on-duty car accident two years prior where I was t-boned in my police car leaving me with a herniated disk, chronic pain and the first of two life-altering on duty concussions, the baby decided he didn't want a natural arrival, opting for a dramatic emergency C-section.

My milk came in late due to the C-section so we had a hungry baby who ended up jaundiced. He had to be tube fed by my amazing husband while my milk came in. Thank God my mother, who is a retired health nurse, drove all night long from Vernon to be there for the birth and became my advocate because I turned into a pile of mush. After returning home from the hospital I had an infection caused by a painful, clogged breast duct. This had to be drained with a giant needle back at the hospital. I then had to feed on that side again because I felt shamed if I didn't continue to breastfeed. I wanted to quit, but I had been trained to push through. This stoic quality was an asset for policing.

I wanted to continue so badly that although my nipples were a mess I purchased a nipple shield, much to the dismay of the nurse who did our first home visit.

Finally after months, we left the house. I could whip the nipple shield out and get ready to feed like a sharp shooter. We would end up nursing in the bathroom at yoga class, crying together.

I don't know who cried more, me or him. Nothing would help to soothe him. Other moms would come in to do a quick feed and happily go back to class. We would leave yoga defeated and embarrassed driving the forty minutes home where he would sleep like a log again. I cried. I felt like a complete failure as a mom. I just wanted to go back to work.

Twelve months later I was back at work and used my coffee breaks to pump. I had to take off my bullet proof vest and hide the pump under my shirt while listening to the police radio.

After two years balancing my police work and being a new mom, we were blessed with a second baby and I went off on parental leave thinking I was way more equipped this time round.

One day I put my newborn down for a nap then went to wake my eldest son for our one-to-one big brother bonding time. I walked into the hall and was shocked to see the baby gate was open and so was the front door. Wide open.

I frantically ran outside and started screaming his name. No answer.

The carnage, the dead bodies, the smells, the accidents, the cries of people losing loved ones, the cries for help. I'd been able to be stoic for the people and the communities I've served, and the calls I've taken and investigated, especially the ones that I carry with me and can no longer outrun, but nothing could have prepared me for that one moment of sheer terror.

Our street was curved around the side of a mountain. I couldn't see down the road and I couldn't see my son anywhere. There were no sidewalks and if you walked far enough you would end up on the highway.

This was my worst nightmare.

All I could think of was, "Am I the mom who lost her child? No wait, am I the cop who lost her child?"

I ran inside to see if he was hiding in the house somewhere. Nothing. Only silence.

I heard a woman's voice. She was walking up the driveway toward the front door holding my son by the hand. My son, so young, bright and naive about the dangers that lurked everywhere, the ones I took an oath to protect him from, had directed her to our home. She had seen him without a jacket, in the cold weather alone, and brought him back. A complete stranger had saved me.

Every emotion flooded me. Joy, shame, embarrassment, relief, anger, all at the same time. I ran over to him and hugged him so tight, tears in my eyes, of joy realizing that in that moment I almost lost a piece of my heart, myself, my soul.

This is what it must feel like to be on the other side of the call. I wasn't the cop at that moment. I was the mother. I had lost (and found) the most precious thing in my life. My child. Someone I had at one time thought I never wanted.

There may be no more piña coladas on the beach on my days off, but I wear my working mother title with pride. I can do both, I can be both.

———

Natasha is currently taking a break from policing to study acting. She's the mom of three to Camden, Kellen and Adelyn, and was a teenage figure skating pro with Disney on Ice. Her dream vacation would include walking miles of fine sugar sand by crystal blue waters with a good pina colada in hand. Cover your ears, Natasha can often be heard saying, 'What the fuck?' And really, who could disagree?

Natasha Bruce

lostandfoundmommy.com
natashanicole47

Courtney

♥

Ultra-Mom

I stood up and felt a warm trickle down my leg. Crap, I thought, I am peeing myself. I took a step towards the front door and a liquid that was not pee gushed out of me. It was like every time I had looked down and all of my toenails were gone...shit happens.

With each movement I made, fluid just kept pouring out of me. Uhm...what do I do?! Why won't it stop? Confused, surprised and a little panicked, I just stood there looking down at my running shoes, watching what I assumed was amniotic fluid, gush onto the floor. I was thirty-eight-weeks pregnant.

My first thought was, damnit did I just ruin my favourite pair of running shorts? My second thought was towels...lots of towels... I quickly shuffled my feet through the large puddle, and back to the stairs. Gripping the railing, I pulled myself up one step at a time, leaving a trail of water behind me. I made it back up to the kitchen, grabbed all the dishtowels I could, stuffed them into my shorts, and sat on a chair. My intro to the world of diapers.

Well I guess this is it, I thought. Without a doubt, labour had begun, and motherhood was inevitable. My biggest fears were now in motion. I was nervous and scared, but I was ready, I had to be.

I sat in that chair waiting for some sort of lightning bolt of pain to overcome my body, wondering what was next, and why it was taking so long for my husband to get home. My only expectation was that this was going to hurt...a lot. I assumed it would be more painful than pulling tape off of open chafe wounds, or would it be more like waking up on day five of a seven-day race? Although I was more nervous than I had ever been before, I sat calmly. My mind drifted... bringing me to every start line I had ever toed.

I had expressed my nerves with a friend at work and what she said never left me, "Why are you scared about labour, you'll be fine! You know, you've done runs longer than you will be in labour." I laughed. It was true, but I had spent the previous nine months dreading this moment. I couldn't imagine giving birth. Though I'd run up mountains in the snow and darkness completely alone, I felt totally unprepared for what was about to happen. Labour and motherhood I feared more than anything else.

For me, running is life. The choice to run is easy, the act of running is what I have dedicated my life to. I progressed naturally from half-marathons to marathons, to wondering what was next. I was a little too comfortable running my first marathon. Deep into my first 50k, with no idea what I was doing, suffering out there in the mountains, I knew I wanted to get to the finish line more than I wanted to stop. I kept moving one foot in front of the other, as uncomfortable as it was. A few minutes after I crossed the finish line, I heard there was going to be an option to run 130kms the following year. In that moment, I decided I was going to do it. I had entered the world of ultrarunning. The word ultra means: going beyond what is usual or ordinary; excessive; extreme. It is by definition, me.

Twenty-seven hours into labour I was kneeling on the bed. I was crazy thinking I wanted to give birth like this but nonetheless I was kneeling. I had seen someone in a prenatal class video giving birth in this position. It was supposed to help reduce the chances of tearing which sounded good to me! The next contraction struck, I took a deep inhale from the gas mask, and realized it was time to push. I had screamed through the contractions but this one in particular scared the shit out of me because I was still terrified of pushing. I didn't tell anyone I felt the urge to push. Instead I shifted to lying on my back, and there it was again. Unfortunately, not pushing during childbirth is not an option.

After each push I blacked out. I could still hear what was going on around me, but I laid still in darkness. It was euphoric, something I was familiar with. My mind often leaves my physical body when I reach a certain distance or time while running. All the physical pain and any doubts I am feeling disappear. My mind takes control and everything I am doing becomes pure bliss. I describe it as the place where my mind connects to my heart. For me this is where my true self lives, and when I get to spend time with her.

I heard a voice in the distance say, "Come on, Courtney you can do this, you're halfway up the grouse grind!"

I laughed, silently. The grouse grind is my morning coffee. If only she knew all of the ultras I had run. I was trained to endure this. Pushing as hard as I could, I heard my husband eagerly say, "Babe I can see the head, you're almost there!"

I thought, "I fucking know!!! I can feel it!!!" And then, I felt my body open, slowly, and a release of pressure. I felt our baby enter the world.

His warm body lay on my chest. The world was moving quickly around us and as we lay still, I stared at his face. All at once I had crossed one finish line and started another.

Ultrarunning has a way of chewing you up and spitting you out. Each time, you emerge a stronger and better person. I endured labour and began motherhood the same way I approach a race. Nervous and excited with a hint of just go for it. I whisper to myself, run your own race.

I said no to an epidural because I wanted to experience every inch of my first child's birth, even though I was terrified. I wanted to feel my baby enter the world. I wanted to find out if my mind and body were capable. I wanted my body to hurt so badly that the strength of my mind could take over and be tested. I don't want to just run. I want to run ultras. I want all of my toenails to fall off, I want to chafe until my skin bleeds.

In the preliminary phases of visualizing a dream or idea, if my mind brings up the word 'can't' or the phrase 'I don't know if I can,' I know I will do it, or at least dedicate myself to trying. I will take on that challenge because I have discovered that's where personal growth flourishes. The dark uncomfortable places of possibility that many do not allow themselves to go to.

I run ultras so any ounce of guilt I have for wanting to be me can wash away. I want my kids to know that their mom is crazy, like everyone says, but she doesn't believe in the word can't. I run ultras because I want to show others that moms are capable and strong. That as moms we have to fight to keep who we are alive, and it's really hard, but we can do it!

After fifteen hours of running, I look forward to another ten because I am free, I am strong, I am covered head to toe in dirt and sweat and it's my most authentic self.

Running ultras is a choice, changing diapers is not and I do not have to change any diapers while running an ultra.

10... 9... 8... 7... I turn around, peering through the crowd of fellow racers to see James, his excited eyes and cheeks, wide with a smile, in the arms of my husband. They are waving together and shouting, "Bye Mommy." I fight back tears. Navigating motherhood and running ultras, mean everything to me; I give every ounce of myself to each of them every day.

6... 5... 4... 3... I turn back around looking up at the trail in front of me, not a single dirty diaper in sight.

2... 1... Ultra-Mom.

Courtney 43

Courtney is a mom of two who has built her personal life and career around physically challenging herself and others as a pipeline to personal growth. Courtney's heart beats best when she is running loooooooong distances. She's happiest covered in mud, hours from home, running up a mountain. Which is one reason it's surprising how much she dislikes showering.

Courtney McQueen

runlikeagirl.ca
🔲 runlikeagirl_ca
🔲 courtney_rlag

Vanessa

♥

With Love.

My first memory of my mother is her lying on the ground. A short while later, an ambulance took her away. It's quite possible this stands out for me not because of the shock — though it was indeed shocking — but because it happened so often that the image is burned into my memory, like when you stare at the sun too long.

My mom's suicide attempts will always be a part of my life, and I suppose because it happened so frequently, they became normalized. As a kid, I didn't understand her condition. Growing up without a stable mother figure had its effect in myriad ways: not trusting, not having a mom I could rely on, not being like other kids, not having the same things, the same food, or any of the same experiences. The Ministry of Child Services was involved in our lives for as long as I can remember.

My mom had untreated bi-polar disorder, a misdiagnosis of schizophrenia, and in all likelihood, postpartum depression. She would express all her sadness to me — crying and lamenting life – and the next thing I knew, she'd be leaving on a stretcher.

But there were ups to go with the downs — the manic stuff I didn't quite understand as a child. And those up times were great, because they were so incredibly fun — at least when I was younger. My mother was happiest when she was singing karaoke and dancing around the living room, sometimes spinning my sister and I as though we were on a ballroom dance floor. She would close her eyes and lose herself in song as she belted out the lyrics, the way you do in the shower, or driving down the highway. Her jubilance was contagious, too. She'd always get my little sister worked up and the two of them together were absolutely hilarious.

My mom also loved — I mean LOVED — Barbie dolls. My dad stayed home, as part of a court order that my sister and I not be left alone with my mother, and took care of us while she went to work at a low paying job. Any extra money she had she'd save up and buy Barbies for Chantel and me — for birthdays, holidays, just randomly. She loved getting down on the floor with us and playing with them. Anytime. She may have loved them more than we did. Dressing them up, acting out happy families and romantic love stories, was easy for her.

My sister and I were ALWAYS a priority for her, THE priority, unlike me — I always believe I have too much on my plate to indulge my kids in that sort of play for very long. Mom did it effortlessly and enthusiastically. She came up with long, elaborate stories about each doll, and each had her own personality. Playing make-believe was never boring to her, in fact, it seemed like she never wanted it to end.

But most of us get past the stage of Barbies, and my teenage years were full of resentment and embarrassment. I vowed that I would never, ever, be anything like my mother. I saw her mental illness as a devastating weakness. I saw her as weak. I grew to hate her.

And yet I loved her.

In an effort to deal with her emotions and, I assume, the fact that few people truly understood her — her illness, uniqueness, and eccentricities — my mom wrote a lot. Songs and poetry. She would often sing or read to us. Story after story after story. She would read to us until we were asleep, and later as I got older, she'd read to me while I was in the tub. It soothed me to hear her voice outside the bathroom door. 'My Child,' is a song she wrote and always sang to me. I can still hear her sweet voice singing...

> *"...You are my child forever you'll be*
> *but when you grow up I'll set you free*
> *while you are young you'll stay with me.*
> *We are so close you and I,*
> *I never want to say goodbye..."*

Now that I have my own kids — and any mother can relate — it's such an intense feeling to have children who exist in this world, a part of but separate from you. The love we have for our children is deep and profound.

That's why she was never successful in taking her life. Until she was.

When we were little, she couldn't fully give up because we needed her. But after my dad's death when I was in my mid-teens, she saw that I could take care of my sister, and everything changed. Our relationship experienced a downward spiral and she moved out, or rather, I pushed her out. She got an apartment and gave "life outside of motherhood," a shot. We did not realize it then but we were her "life."

Mom died when I was twenty and Chantel was sixteen.

The first thing we saw when we entered her apartment were the Barbies. At least twenty, maybe thirty, all laid out looking beautiful. She had dressed each one and brushed out their hair. It looked like a little girl had been there for hours preparing her dolls for a big soirée. All around them she had spread out her good-bye songs and poems.

Her death brought on a lot of mixed emotions, including relief, because I knew she was no longer in pain. Overwhelmingly, however, I felt resentment. I convinced myself that her suicide wasn't intentional. That it was just another cry for help and she didn't mean for it to go that far. That she had screwed up. I was so angry for so long. Instead of having compassion, I had thought, "How stupid of her, because this time it actually worked and she couldn't take it back."

It wasn't until summer of 2020, almost two decades later, when I re-read her poems and goodbye notes through a different lens that I finally saw her completely. While I don't have the same mental health struggles, I could finally see her as a mother, and the hell she must have been going through. I finally understood that she really had thought everything through. She fully intended on succeeding at her suicide that last time. It brought about a big explosion of emotions when I realized Mom had finally reached her breaking point. It wasn't a cry for help. She intended to be successful.

I've spent the last year diving into personal and spiritual work and developed a deep appreciation for who my mom was and the suffering she endured. I forgave her for not being the person I thought she needed to be, and I came to love and respect her for being who she was.

I grew up wanting to become an independent, determined, strong, successful woman, in spite of who I thought my mother was. Today, I would describe myself as exactly that. And I now see that I inherited these qualities from my mom. It's official, I became the woman I vowed my whole life never to be anything like.

I loved her, I hated her, I lost her, and then I became her.

I became that woman I dreamed of being. But I became that woman *thanks* to my mom. I became a powerful, passionate, fearless woman, *because of her*, not in spite of her. She did everything, and I mean everything, with love. I vow to live each day, with my own children, doing the same.

I think of her now, and whisper, "God, if I could just give her one more hug." If I could just tell her that I get it. Now, I get it. I get it.

If Vanessa had a Saturday without her six-year-old twins, she'd browse, have a nice lunch and listen to podcasts. But really, she'd rather be at her camp, with her staff and campers. Any day. EVERY day! Camp is life! Working with children, specifically girls, Vanessa helps them live their best lives, love themselves, and create strong 'sister' bonds where girls hold each others' hands 'to the top.' LOVE IT!!! Gosh, I truly wish I could be at camp all day every day!!

Vanessa Doak

🅞 healthyheartsbc

🅞 withlovebc

♥

Pep Talk:
Put the Dang Suit On

F L A W S O M E // adj. A rad woman who embraces her "flaws" and knows she's awesome regardless.

Because celebrating every-BODY is something I can really get be-HIND.

Size six or sixteen, our little ones just want us in the pool, not on the sidelines. We've got babes to inspire so I'm getting out there with every fold, dimple and stretch mark.

Do us a favour...be brave and put the suit on!

Motherhood comes in every shape, size and struggle. No two journeys are the same, so own it. You're one in a big beautiful juicy melon.

Sun's out, cheeks out!

Christina + Carolyn

♥

The Same Love

I strode down the sidewalk and into a café noting that everyone I passed was giving me a longer than usual look. *How do all of these strangers know how different I feel right now?* Out in public for the first time since becoming a mother I stood in line to order feeling emotionally exposed. Enjoying the smell of roasted coffee, I felt a cool sensation on my chest, I glanced down. My boob was hanging out of my top.

The whole world couldn't see my soul, they could see my boob!

After a few weeks together at home with our newborn baby my partner left for work abroad. The eight weeks he was away were grueling. I was a zombie who, looking back, probably shouldn't have been behind the wheel of a car. This baby stuff was bananas! As the weeks progressed, I came to a very firm conclusion: I could not be a single parent. The affirmation somehow helped pull me through each endless day, knowing I was one day closer to my partner's return.

Family on both sides helped and it was only because of them that I ate nutritious food and kept my sanity. As a reward for this trial by fire I scheduled a pedicure for the day after his arrival. I daydreamed about having my dried husks of feet rejuvenated and, most importantly, a few precious hours to myself without worry.

When my partner arrived home, my sense of security and safety returned, and the next day I stepped out into the world away from my tiny sidekick. It felt wondrous and strange. A new quality of freedom I had never experienced before. I nearly skipped out the door. I had kept my baby alive through acrobatic feats of feeding and sleep deprivation. *Everything's okay now.*

Returning home after a blissful date with myself, smelling of nail polish and already missing my baby, I found the two of them sitting in a chair in the nursery. There was a seriousness in the room that shifted my mood to high alert. I stood there in shock and listened to him speak, "Not wanting this... should've broken up... deeply regretful... one week on, one week off..." Less of a conversation, more of a revelation. As if on cue our child started crying but my heart beat so loudly in my ears I hardly noticed. The room felt hot, dark, and suddenly claustrophobic.

"Are we breaking up?" I asked.

At first, I refused to believe it. Then, I was pissed. I was furious with him, with all men. A rage that was not only mine made me mean. Later I would bargain, trying my best to come to an agreement that would help us both, a scenario where I wasn't alone with this responsibility. The more I tried to make sense of what was happening, the deeper I fell into quicksand until I was nearly suffocating. And there I stayed, with just my head poking out, trying not to sink deeper. Knowing that if I did, I would be crushed completely.

Somehow I believed I deserved to be abandoned. No matter how many different perspectives I tried in order to let myself off the hook, I always arrived at the same conclusion. I must be unlovable. Looking in the mirror most days I would assess myself, *I'm not doing okay. Should I ask someone for help? Do I need to go to a doctor?* Then I'd place a suit of mental armour carefully over top of the broken, gooey mess that I was and face the world.

Meanwhile, something unusual was unfolding in my day-to-day life. For a person who considered herself to be an awkward, self-conscious introvert I was surprised by my desire to connect and socialize with other moms. I wanted to not only forge friendships but to help. Sometimes my inner critic would pipe up and say, "You? Helping others? You can barely make it through the day!" But I *was* making it. By connecting with other moms, offering support and accepting their friendship, I grew stronger. Their strength and their stories gave me strength and I could see that motherhood is damn hard and everyone struggles.

What I've learned since is that women are predisposed to respond to stress by nurturing, caring and forging friendships, as opposed to defaulting to that fight or flight narrative we're all familiar with. The female version of MMA fighting is a bunch of caregivers gathered together for coffee with babies in their arms, sharing, laughing, supporting each other so that we can survive, so that our children survive, and the human race can go on. No big deal.

Building connections brought me relief and fortitude. When I was home alone with my daughter I could be curious instead of grief-stricken. There had to be something I was missing, or not understanding that would help to explain the painful situation I was in. I wasn't a monster or a person who did horrible things, so why was this happening? I immersed myself in books and podcasts on relationships and how to improve them but they didn't give me the answers I knew I needed. Like a bloodhound on a scent trail I persisted, learning all I could about personal healing.

One evening, while listening to yet another spiritual leader, Byron Katy, share her wisdom, I put down the dishes and quietly crept upstairs to do the exercise she was explaining in her audiobook. It was a guided examination of a thought that was dominating and tormenting my mind. I went through the steps, not expecting much, just wanting to learn and grow and… WHAM! It was like I had been body checked by a rugby-playing angel. Nearly falling off the bed I slowly went through the exercise again and, profoundly, arrived at the same conclusion. The Answer. A Belief. I didn't *really* love myself.

The brave façade I had worked tirelessly to maintain shattered. Tears came and didn't stop. I lay on my bed trembling from the force. A wild swirl of grief, relief, connection, and sadness engulfed me. I felt as though I was waking up to something the Universe had wanted me to see for a long, long time. "I see it now," I whispered over and over again. I finally understood how the world which exists in our own minds can be reflected in our 4D reality. Clarity.

I had always sat around waiting to be loved but obviously my deep feminine heart had grown weary of this and now there were neon flashing arrows pointing me towards the truth. Having a child proved to me that my heart was built to love fiercely and without limits. Tapping into the energy of my womb, the creative centre of my being, I listened. *Welcome home*, she said. She told me to reclaim the power of love, to first unleash it onto myself and then let it out into the world, to whoever stands before me.

Like a black and white photo that gradually regained its colour, the relationship with my partner improved. I could finally have compassion and respect for the internal challenges he had faced as parenthood confronted him too. More joy found its way into the present moment; my future transformed into something hopeful, and the quicksand released me from its grip.

I had read somewhere whilst pregnant that birth is one of those initiatory events in a woman's life. She must face her darkest shadows beforehand, otherwise they will come forward to be reckoned with. Naively I had assumed my 'work' was to accept my complicated health challenges during pregnancy and delivery. Little did I know there was something much bigger waiting in the wings.

I believe that our perceptions of the world are a reflection of what's going on inside us, the messages running through our subconscious minds. Only when I stopped and peered inward could I begin to change these and unlock the chamber where my transformation would occur. For me the most profound shifts came when I connected to my feminine body, what I believe to be the source of a woman's power, and when it returned, my menstrual cycle. I have a daily spiritual and mindful practice borne out of being attuned to it and celebrating it as my connection to truth, power, nature and love.

"Mommy, I have a secret to tell you," Autumn, my two-year-old daughter said one day. We were at home in the entryway putting shoes and jackets on. I squatted down, and she lifted up the hair over my ear and whispered, "I love you."

―――――

In a perfect, COVID-free world, Melissa would sit on a white sandy beach in Thailand ordering meals to her cabana. She wants to help shift humanity's current course of environmental destruction to one of sustainability and restoration by helping people understand the value of living in a cyclical way. She stress eats but also stress exercises so it kinda balances out.

Melissa Woehler

🄾 melissawoehler

Suzie

I Get to Decide!

My life has been a never-ending game of comparison, with society telling me what to do.

Graduate high school and go to university.

Be married in my twenties.

Be a mom in my thirties.

Society says, I should basically have my shit together and be living the perfect life with the two point five children, the nice SUV, and the beautiful home in a cozy community, with curated photos when I approach my forties.

Growing up I felt I was always compared to others. Whether it was to my big family of siblings, cousins or friends, my whole life was measured or critiqued.

"What about you Suzie? Are you dating anyone?"

I felt people staring when I'd show up at functions, by myself, while everyone else had a partner with them.

I experienced a long term abusive and toxic relationship, a few different jobs, and "friends" who never really understood me. I felt lost and out of control. I was tired of feeling hurt, I knew I wanted more, and deep down I knew I was *worth* more. I needed help. It was scary, but for the first time in my life I was ready to invest and focus on me! I decided that I didn't need a boyfriend or a husband to be worth something. I am worth something all on my own. I decided to live my life for me. Do what *I* wanted to do, when *I* wanted to do it. And, if people didn't like it, too bad for them!

My therapist helped me envision myself as happy and free. Free of all the things that others wanted for me. Free to make my dreams come true. That meant giving myself more permission to live my way. I had to love myself more than anything else. Due to my age, I had to let go of the idea of having my own biological children. That was a super hard one to swallow. But maybe, just maybe, I could be a mother somehow in my own way.

At my core, I loved helping people. When I think back to a time when I felt my proudest it was when I was a lifeguard and experienced a child with special needs refusing to go into the pool. His mom had somehow got him onto the pool deck, kicking and screaming. He was terrified of the water. I knew I could help him. His mom helped me get his fingers uncurled from the fence, he wrapped his arms around my neck, strangling me, and I slowly moved into the pool. The screams became louder before they became better. It took a number of lessons with slow progressions until he felt comfortable enough to release his death grip on my neck.

We eventually were able to get his feet on the bottom of the pool. The tears became less, and the smiles became more. He started to walk, and then jump, slowly discovering that the pool wasn't so bad after all. Over the next month, we were in the water, rain or shine. I taught that little boy how to float. I didn't know it at the time, but it turned out to be one of the most pivotal moments of my life.

I went back to school, completed my degree, and became a teacher.

I continued my counselling and began to determine what I actually wanted. What were my passions? What did I want to do for me? I had to dig deep and give myself permission to explore avenues that had always been closed. I knew that if I ever wanted to really be loved, I needed to love myself.

For my fortieth birthday, I bought myself the gift of a personal trainer. I needed to retrain my body after suffering multiple injuries from car accidents and sport injuries, and I knew that prioritizing my health would help me gain some confidence too.

One afternoon I walked into the gym and there was this nice looking, kind guy there. Somehow, we began to have small conversations as we became more comfortable with one another. The gym became a place of joy for me, having new and different people to socialize with.

One particular workout, he was heading for the front door for a block run and I was riding the stationary bike, reading my book. As he went past me, he said, "If you can read while you're riding, you're not riding hard enough," and chuckled as he went out the door. The bantering moved into long talks on the sidewalk after workouts.

We were married when I was forty-five.

For most of my life I let society define who I was supposed to be. I didn't know any other way. I waited until my forties and fifties and now I'm doing it all! I am an educator, mother, wife, friend, daughter and sister. Many of those titles weren't attained in the conventional way. But guess what, I am not conventional, and I am 100% okay with it.

It has taken me thirty years to get to this point. I give myself grace and I want all women to know and understand that life doesn't have to be conventional. In fact, life IS messy, and I have found magic IN the mess.

There is strength in all of us and I believe as women, we need to share our stories and stick together. We need to follow our passions and celebrate one another. In my twenties, all I wanted was to feel welcome and that I belonged, even though I didn't fit the typical mold.

Occasionally people still say, "Oh, you're not a mom," or other labels that in the past would have upset me, but now I have the confidence to correct them. Now I say, "Actually I am!" Which leads to a question mark on their faces.

Now, I am a mom to forty-five amazing teenage humans, each and every school day. I am a mother to the children who come to school without food. I am a mother who purchases clothing for students in need. I am Momma Sue. I listen, I guide, and I go in and fight some battles with them and for them.

I am also a mother to some staff members. They may be having a rough day and are falling apart. I try to solve whatever problem is going on. Staff I barely know, walk through my door with tears rolling down their faces in frustration and hurt, looking for guidance to solve a situation. Some come to my classroom, sit on a table, and just talk. And, when I see teachers that are working far too many hours and burning out, they get "Bossy Momma Sue." I'll pack up their computer and walk them out the door. It's time for them to go and do something for themselves. They can't keep giving all of themselves away.

I am a Mom without giving birth.

I am a wife to a man who believes in all of me, the messy and the magic.

I am Suzie, fifty-three and living a life that is purposeful, passionate, and fueled with self-love. It took me a long time to get here, but I love where I'm at. Take that Society!

After a busy week as a middle-school teacher Sue enjoys curling up with a book and a glass of red wine. She loves a great thunder and lightning show, almost as much as her collection of coloured pens and post-it notes. Music is powerful and Sue is happy to have it all fill her soul. A good beat, a beautiful memory, a new groove....she'll sing in harmony to just about anything!

Sue Thiessen

⊙ suzie126

♥

Pep Talk:
Pizza! Pizza!

Be loud, be confident, shout it from the drive:thru. You are enough!

Please remember you cannot please everyone, you're not pizza.

So whether you choose take-out or you make the dough from scratch (please teach me how to do this), thin crust, stuffed crust, cheesy crust, gluten free, or extra saucey... pizza is pizza. It doesn't matter which way you slice the pie. This world needs ALL OF YOU.

Remember when McDonald's had pizza? Let's petition it back.

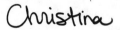

♥

A Life Unzipped

Go ahead...unzip it. Have a look. Inside is everything that makes me who I am. Everything I know, trust and believe. It is the truth I carry. Not visible to the eye but felt deep within the bones of my being.

It is my backpack.

Inside, lives love and joy as well as fear, grief, and deep betrayal. There are lessons from wrong choices, broken relationships, from learning and unlearning, from marriage to motherhood. Some call their backpacks their "baggage," but I see it as a useful tool, a resource I carry. My bag holds my deepest secrets and biggest dreams, and most importantly, the learnings, and the love I have gathered along the way.

If you dig deep enough you will see the big one. The life changing lesson given to me when I was twenty-one. My only parent, my sweet mom Judy who was the most important human in my life, was dying at the age of fifty-three. We spoke openly and often about death...she did her best to prepare me. She promised to always be tucked "in my pocket," looking out for me. I remember joking with her, saying if she was going to be "in my pocket," she should at least make sure I have money in there. We laughed...this was my way of trying to make the heavy conversations a little easier. Moments of lightness, a release from the heartache of watching her suffer.

She was a nurse, an incredibly nurturing human to all, but it was my turn to learn the art of nursing, the craft of preserving her dignity until the end. She lay all tucked in under her favorite white linen. Cancer left her face hollow, her chest a sunken cavity full of sutures, and her gorgeous thick hair replaced with fuzzy grey whisps. But her big blue eyes still sparkled and I made sure her lipstick and blush were intact.

I was young and scared to be left alone with no one to care about me, to love me the way she did. But what she told me that day, has forever stayed in my backpack. She said that while she couldn't make any promises about bringing me money, she would leave me gifts in the form of people. "The most important thing in life is the people you journey with. I will do my best to make sure you always have the right ones."

And, true to her word, she brings me my people. Some only for a short while to add something to my bag or to unzip and share something from theirs. Some come for the sights of that particular part of the adventure. They aren't ready to unzip and that's okay. But some...some stay. They stay for the twists and turns, the road blocks, the bumps and wide open highways. Holding space while I completely unravel, dropping off little gifts just because, or getting me out to have fun. Reminding me I can play despite the pain. These are the ones who join me through the rugged terrain in torrential downpours and the care-free walks on bright sunny days. Only a special few. They stay and they notice, they are curious, they want to know more.

Through the process of unpacking, we come to learn what true connection feels like. That although the contents inside our backpacks may look different, they have been placed inside through experiencing the basic human emotions: joy, anger, sadness, fear, and love. These feelings weave us together with an invisible string, creating the tapestry of our humanity. The process of opening up to others is where I have found real connection...where I found the special few, as promised by my mom.

Recently my backpack became even harder to carry. My son Jude, named after my mom, was diagnosed at the age of four with a rare and fatal degenerative muscle disorder called Duchenne. One spontaneous mutation in his genes means he cannot produce the protein needed to keep his muscles intact. Every day he will lose muscle. Every day his movements become more restricted, his breath more shallow, and his heartbeat weakened. There is no cure. For us, time is muscle.

The gripping fear of what lies ahead is something I feel with each breath, a constant heaviness in this momma's heart. The weight of a million bricks inside my backpack. These heavy belongings bring me into the present moment, reminding me that life holds no promises. To say accepting our son's expiration date is excruciating work is an understatement. I have become very close friends with grief.

The sound of Jude crying as we brace his legs and apply the oxygen mask every night. When he looks up with those familiar blue eyes and says, "This isn't fair, why me?" When we find him in tears because he can't run, jump, or play like the other kids. Grief in feeling freedom in my own movement and wanting that for Jude. Grief with the passing of time. With each day. With each breath.

How do I get unstuck? I have started realizing the only way is to let people in, to share with others what

I am carrying. It's scary, I still catch myself not wanting to bring people down by sharing the tragic pieces of my life. Sometimes the words stay in my throat. I push them out, I know this is where healing happens.

I focus on bringing awareness to what matters most. Getting clear on how I want to spend this sacred time with Jude. I am learning to ask for help. I am learning how to let my heart marinate in the groundlessness of it all...the deep aching that never stops. Slowly, I feel myself move through the stickiness.

I have learned that hope, freedom, and inner peace come less from focusing on what has been handed to me and more from bringing awareness to how I show up in the thick of uncertainty. Some days I feel open-hearted and other days I struggle with the unfairness of it all. But above all else, there is hope.

Human connections are what bring me hope. The love, support, and compassion of friends, family, and people whose faces I have never seen but offer to take a few bricks out of my bag. My light shines because people care. These human connections have not only saved me but have given me the fuel to be in service for others. To continue the ripple.

Just over a year ago, one of my special few, my best friend Maggie and I created something called the MASH movement. Our names, Maggie plus Kasha, together, ready to help others unzip using the values that have helped us. MASH = Movement, Awareness,

Service and Health. We want to bring hope to this world, for my courageous son, and all the other children with Duchenne. We keep bringing people together in physical movement, through yoga and fitness, to raise awareness and funds towards a cure. Working our muscles to create hope for those who are losing theirs.

Our mission isn't just about bringing awareness to the tangible muscles of our bodies, but the muscles of our beings: compassion, empathy, courage, intuition, patience, the muscles of our hearts. These are the ones that help carry the weight of any backpack. These are the ones that create healing. These are the ones that remind people they are not alone.

I have journeyed the rough terrain at the end of life with both loved ones and professionally as a nurse. My takeaway is always the same. A life well lived is a life unzipped. It's confusing when the outside world tells us it's not safe to reveal what we are carrying. It's scary and exhausting. But do it anyway, open those backpacks often, for yourself and for the littles who are watching.

Remember the tools available to us all: kindness, compassion, humour, forgiveness, intuition, courage. Use them all to help keep those backpacks feeling light and to keep you in movement. Adjust your straps, lift your chin and carry your bag with pride. It doesn't have to be perfect. It has to be you. Everything you know, trust, and believe. Believe in connection. Hope will follow. Find your special few, live your MASH.

Kasha is a nurse educator and co-founder of the MASH Movement which raises funds for Duchenne Muscular Dystrophy, the fatal neuromuscular disease one of her children suffers from. Her family is her everything. She cries all the time at movies and commercials but never while she's deep knee bending to Ra Ra Rasputin on the dance floor.

Kasha Mitton

themashmovement.com
📷 themashmovement
🅵 The Mash Movement

Maggie

Home is Where You Are

I've packed and unpacked my bag more times than I can count. I've added and emptied clothes, objects, and feelings. Starting from when I was young and my parents courageously decided to separate. As a teen-ager I adjusted to having to create a sense of home in two places. I would carefully unpack my things between two loving homes to give myself permission to settle in where I was staying. I started to notice that I had one foot in and one foot out. I was living a new norm where uncertainty started to creep in. I ached for the other parent wherever I was sleeping, wondering if I was upsetting them for not being in their home. I started to navigate an overwhelming feeling of loss, and I felt guilty owning this emotion knowing that I was lucky enough to have both my mom and my dad in my life. I stuffed my sadness back in my backpack. I did not want to upset them; my parents loved and supported me unconditionally. I wanted them and my younger siblings to know I was strong, I was okay and I could do this.

As an adult, I decided to pack my bag and follow the love of my life to his home in Toronto. My sadness was shoved to the bottom of my bag leaving behind my family, friends, comfort zone, my love for the outdoors, the fresh mountain air, and laid back lifestyle and would be traded for a new beginning, adventure and the urban, concrete and vibrant jungle.

Each time my bag is thrown on the conveyor belt at the airport so too are the emotions inside it. The feeling of unease, the balancing act of having two homes: B.C. and Ontario. My suitcase carries my joy, adventure, happiness, nerves, grief and connection. It is my invisible container filled with experiences of how I have lived and continue to live, a reminder of the feelings I have buried in the bottom pocket of my bag. Feelings I do not want to burden others with.

There are times I sit at the dinner table surrounded by people who care for me, a table full of joy, laughter, and love. People I am lucky enough to call my new family and who make me feel at home. But these moments come and go and my sense of uncertainty creeps back in. I feel homesick and alone.

Alone.

A word, a sentiment, a state, a thought. Something I think I need to protect myself from feeling.

I have days and months where I feel settled, grounded and stable. I am proud of myself. I won the in-law family lottery, I love my job, I am a part of an amazing yoga community, I volunteer and give back to my community. I am home. And then out of nowhere my world feels turned upside down. There is an ache in my heart for my family, friends, the mountains, and the lifestyle. I think of the snowy peaks and blue ocean and I catch myself still calling B.C. home.

When I first made the move out East, I wasn't aware of how guarded I was, I always considered myself an extrovert, outgoing and comfortable walking into a room full of people I didn't know and striking up a conversation. But what I have realized is that I wasn't always willing to unzip my backpack, I didn't want my new friends to see me in pain and to feel unseen themselves. Something held me back from unzipping, from talking about my loneliness. I wasn't ready to share the contents I carried and held so tightly. Maybe I wasn't ready to unpack and allow space for new items, experiences, or even feelings to fit inside.

With time and in movement, I have recognized something about myself: that I hold my family and friends in high regard and sometimes prevent myself from making new and close connections with others. I am not sure if that is a fear that my people will be forgotten, or worse yet that I will be forgotten. I don't know if it's because deep down I feel this is not my forever home and I am not sure I can bear to ache for more people in my life, should that move back West take place. If I don't risk making new friendships I won't have to say goodbye again.

What I do have is my passion and call to action to be of service for those in my family, in my community, and to complete strangers. My move out East initiated a journey of self-awareness. It taught me that I am brave, strong, and I belong. I have made lasting and deep connections with my yoga community and have been able to connect my worlds from west to east through yoga classes and fundraisers.

Sometimes I sit with an emotional rollercoaster of confusion asking myself if where I am is where I need to be. What I am aware of, is how my own acts of service have created an ability for me to stand in my true north, ground my feet, and feel that I am exactly where I need to be.

And just when I start to feel rooted in my new territory something happens, something shifts, a family member back home is in need or a picture of a reunion has been posted and I feel split in half again.

The journey of life and motherhood has brought me so much love, joy, gratitude, and also anxiety. Motherhood has taught me that I have more love than I ever thought I could carry, hold, and give. With this unconditional and infinite love I find myself gasping for air in the uncertainty of knowing whether I am doing it right, whether I am where I need to be? Wondering what my kids' lives would look like if we were living in B.C.? Wondering what it feels like for my mom and dad being so far away from their grandchildren? Wondering if I would miss my new home, family and friends from Ontario like I do for B.C.?

As a mother *I am* committed to sharing with my young, naive, and tenacious kids the value in being vulnerable and I know this begins with me modelling for them. I am comfortable crying in front of them and talking about sadness, and my hope is that as they get older they will be comfortable truly feeling one another's pain and embracing each other's joy. Feeling for others is what has set my relationships apart. From acquaintances to kindreds. This openness gives me permission to unpack my bag and create space for new contents, feelings, connections, and for new roots to be planted.

As I watch my own children grow in a beautiful, safe, and loving environment, a place so far away from where I grew up, I am thankful that their home and their backpacks are being filled with laughter, love, play, and opportunities. I watch them begin to create their own connections. I am thrilled for them. I am thrilled this is their home. And I am sad that my old home is not theirs.

What I want them to know is that it's safe for them to unzip and unpack their bags here. That unzipping is where they will find true connection and purpose. They have gifted me a new perspective of home. They give me permission to unpack and to pack my suitcase over and over again. I have learned that my home is where they are.

It's not just about the lessons, but about WHO the lessons are shared with. And that the WHO might not always be physically with you but that movement, awareness and service to one another can always bring you home.

Alone I am Maggie. But together, we are family.

The healing journey is deeply personal...but nobody said you have to do it alone.

———

Sydney and Hudson's mama is an elementary school teacher who loves hot sweaty power yoga and long nature walks with an audiobook. She is co-founder of the MASH Movement and is on a mission to raise awareness and find a cure for Duchenne Muscular Dystrophy. Maggie would be lost without her family, friend hangouts, and venti blonde roast with cream and cinnamon.

Maggie Aynsley

themashmovement.com
🅾 themashmovement
🅵 The Mash Movement

♥

Pep Talk:
Choose YOU!

As moms we often think, *Oh, I just don't have time for myself!* But really that needs to shift to giving ourselves the permission to ask, *What do I need right now?*

Manicures, haircuts, an hour ALONE with no one touching you, and a clean playroom can make us feel good, but self care is more than "feel good" moments. It's a conscious *connection* to the thing you are doing and to the thing that you need.

Choosing to put yourself at the top of the list and then advocating for it. This is self care.

Choosing YOU is mandatory.

We always have a choice. Here's your permission slip to say yes to yourself, your needs, wants, and desires. Start with ten minutes per day.

You deserve this.

Carolyn

Carly

♥

The Birthday Letter

Dear Carly,

Tomorrow my darling, is your thirty-second birthday and by the end of it, everything will change. There is nothing you can do to prepare for what will come next. No answers or analysis. No amount of good karma or bad horoscopes can make you ready for the heartache of loss. Of grief. Of crumbling. And then rediscovering, as if it was for the very first time, the person you see in the mirror — proud, confident and worthy.

That person looking back at you will be the woman, the mother, you were always meant to be.

But first, the loss.

It will feel like any other birthday as a parent, the usual 6 a.m. wake up, lukewarm coffee, a messy house, red velvet cake. You will go for a family walk on a day that is so sunny it has no business being in April. You will look ahead to see your husband and two-year-old daughter walking hand-in-hand, and you will feel your throat tighten. This will be the last walk you will take together as a family.

That evening will also be the beginning of the end of your dad's life. You knew the cancer was back, but you thought you had more time. We always think we have more time.

You will go to the hospital every day for a month. Sometimes Dad will be angry, sometimes he will cry, sometimes he won't know who you are. You will be there, holding his hand, when he takes his final breath.

In the same month you are losing your dad, you will also lose your marriage.

The end of your eleven-year relationship will come fast and slowly at the same time. Part of you saw it coming during the counselling, but stubborn "*I can fix anything*" Carly refused to listen (as you often do). You were so busy achieving and taking care of everything so he would choose you, when really, you needed to choose you.

The months that come next will be a painful, but necessary evil. Writing a eulogy and planning a funeral will be tough, potty training will be tougher. You will drink too much. You will learn what all the kids are talking about swiping left and right, but those will be temporary distractions. *Spoiler alert* — do NOT go for drinks with Stan. You will lean on people who love you, spend a small fortune on therapy, and develop an anxiety disorder. You will feel shame when you have to ask for help.

The morning of Dad's funeral you will attempt your makeup (for the third time) and pause to stare in the mirror - the woman you will see is not a woman at all. She is a little girl. She is broken. She has lost two people she loved. You won't recognize her.

While your husband packs his things a look of confusion will cross your daughter's face. Your time away from her will feel like another loss, as she is shared between two homes, sleeping in two beds. You will feel a paralyzing guilt for failing your family, for failing as a mother.

You will grieve the family vacations you'll never take, the home you worked so hard to create, the second baby you thought you might have one day. Small dreams and big dreams will be ripped from under you. The future will be unclear.

As you learn what it means to co-parent you will also learn what it means to sit with yourself. Alone. The peaceful Saturday morning sleep-ins and warm coffees you always dreamt about, will instead be the most dreaded day of the week. The house will be quiet. But your heart will not. You miss your family. You miss your dad. You miss Carly.

Some days you will play *Frozen* on repeat and lay on the couch trying to hide the tears from your daughter. You won't sleep. You'll lose weight, not the healthy kind. Thank goodness for the people who keep reminding you of your strength, even though you feel anything but strong.

Most of all, you will feel intense guilt for being a career-woman — questioning every decision you ever made. Going back to work after four weeks of mat leave. Working sixty-hour weeks in the early days of the business. Moving the office out of your home to grow the team. The list goes on. You will wonder, if you had given up your business, would your marriage have survived?

People will say, your daughter is young, she won't *remember*, and it's better this way. These comments make it worse. Coming from a divorced family, the only thing you ever wanted was for your daughter to have the opposite. She won't remember when you were all together, when her parents loved each other. She won't remember. But you will.

As a recovering perfectionist you will hate the lack of control this season brings. You will read all the books. You will sit in pain. You will write. You will also lose your grandmother. There's the three. Three things to grieve while running a business and raising a two year old, in the middle of a pandemic.

But know this, brave girl, you do this. One day at a time, little by little, you will be brought closer to meeting the next version of yourself. And there's so much to be grateful for. A thriving, healthy daughter. The best year of business to date. A group of friends who show up for you. A family who becomes closer than ever before.

One by one these people, these moments will help you rise. You will learn it's okay to ask for help, to let go of control, to be imperfect. You will find your voice.

There will be new-found peace in your co-parenting life. Being the best divorced parent is, of course, top of your list. Family walks are still to come, just as a different kind of family now. Forgiveness will feel powerful.

You will walk into your office with confidence, feeling true ownership and pride in the business you created. No more guilt. No more feeling like you have to be this *or* that. A working mom *or* a stay at home mom. Successful in your career *or* successful in your home. You can be both. You are providing for your daughter.

You are leading a team of women. You are an incredible mother. You are both.

You will still be scared, often. But you will not let the fear lead you.

And perhaps most unexpectedly, beautiful girl, you will fall in love again. When you're busy healing and learning and growing, he will show up. Some guy will be parked in your stall at the office, you will leave a passive-aggressive note, share a few uncomfortable elevator rides and eventually creep each other on Instagram. He'll remind you what it means to feel joy, to be seen, and to be supported.

You will remember what it feels like to learn new things and be excited about your life. To dream new dreams. To trust and be inspired. To redefine motherhood, on your own terms.

One night, not far from your thirty-third birthday, you will be finishing up your daughter's bath time and find yourself again in that damn mirror. This time you're not alone. Wrapped in your arms in her pink unicorn towel, your daughter will place both hands on your cheeks, stare you straight in the eye and say, *"Mumma, are you happy?"*

So much has changed. But there is always love. You will be okay, and she will be okay, because you are her mom. Don't be scared. This messy year, this unplanned chapter is called *living*. As tears stream down your face you will bring her in close and whisper, "*Yes, my darling, I'm happy.*"

———

As founder and creative director of White Canvas Design Studio, an all female creative marketing agency, Carly is passionate about empowering women and moms in the workplace. She was a hotshot softball player on the Junior Women's National Team and attended SFU on an athletic scholarship. Carly swears a lot, but is working on it because you know, toddlers.

Carly Moir

whitecanvasdesign.ca
whitecanvasdesignstudio

Chrissy

♥

Fat

I was fat. Morbidly obese doctors called it. Whenever I would see a commercial for that awful show where they do exposés on 600 pound people my heart would skip a beat. "That is going to be me."

I had just turned forty and I thought my life was over. Is this all there is for me? How do I begin to fix this? I would get so overwhelmed thinking of this, I would eat more food to make myself feel better and to ignore my problems for a little while longer. Tomorrow, I would tell myself, I'll figure it out tomorrow.

My cycle of using food for comfort began very early in life. Some of my first memories are of hiding chocolate chips under our couch. Even at five years old, I knew it was shameful to eat too much. What started as a sneaky habit grew into a full blown addiction. To fuel this, I would drive to multiple fast food restaurants, order food for people who didn't exist at each one, and go home by myself to eat it all. I ate until I was so full I felt sick, then waited just long enough so I could eat more.

When I had roommates, I would say no to social events so I could stay home and eat alone. Always in secret. Actually, that's not true. Sometimes I would cultivate friendships with other bingers and we would eat together. Call it quality time.

I have shattered plastic deck chairs, had trouble buckling airplane seatbelts on the largest setting, and once had to tell a room full of people, some friends, some I had only met the night before, that I couldn't go ziplining when offered a free trip because I was too heavy. At that point I was over 275 pounds. The moment was one of the final straws that kickstarted me to get healthy.

Being fat wasn't just affecting my social life it was taking a huge toll on my family as well. Every day I was isolating more and more. I would rather stay home alone than go to the park or for a walk, or anywhere for that matter. I blamed it on being a mom, that taking care of two kids was exhausting, and I was exhausted, but not because my kids were difficult. I woke up every day feeling like shit because I had stayed up late eating junk food. I was so riddled with shame because of it that I lashed out at everyone around me. Including my kids. My house was full of yelling and chaos and none of us were having a good time. By the time my oldest started kindergarten my behaviour couldn't be hidden any longer. In her first year she missed a total of twenty days of school because I couldn't get myself together enough to take her and she was late over a hundred times.

I had been trapped my entire life by this addiction. I had tried and successfully lost weight in the past, but it always came back with more. I had done all the diets: Slim Fast, Weight Watchers, green coffee pills, low carb, no fat, and even some mystery liquid I bought off the internet that claimed to "melt the fat away." Spoiler, it didn't.

I know that social media isn't perfect but I am going to credit Facebook for helping me save my life. Right when I needed it, I began seeing posts from my friend Holly, who I hadn't spoken to in over twenty years. She was working with a health coach and she was killing it! I watched and read everything she posted and was enraptured by it. She wasn't talking about her exercise or her food, she talked about her self-esteem, her love for her body and her life!

This was my first introduction to Project Healthy Body. I cyber stalked founder Jennifer Joffe and when I read her story, I wept. Once obese herself, here was a woman who got me and what it felt like to be a food addict, binge eater and how being overweight negatively effected every aspect of my life. I begged her to take me on as a client.

If I wanted to love my life, she said, I needed to first love myself. I had no idea what that even meant and truthfully the term made me cringe. I knew I didn't love myself, quite the opposite actually. Learning that self-love isn't just positive affirmations, though we do those too, it is built from how we treat ourselves, was a lifeline I eagerly reached for. It made perfect sense to me as the worse I treated myself the worse I felt about myself. So, it stood to reason that if I began to treat myself better, I would also feel better.

While it may not seem very wild and sexy it was the most profound journey I have ever embarked on. Loving myself as I am now so I can do the work to be the person I know I am meant to be. This is how I went from self-loathing to self love and I lost 120 pounds along the way. I want to be crystal clear. I didn't love myself because I lost weight, I lost weight because I learned how to love and care for myself.

I ate whole real food, ditched the processed garbage junk food that was poisoning my body and mind, drank water and walked around my neighbourhood. I got real about my role in everything, and got in touch with my emotions. Feeling things has always been hard for me and an ongoing process in order to break my emotional eating patterns. I changed my routines from unhealthy to healthy ones. I lost weight the same way I will keep it off, by building systems which support being a healthy person. No quick fixes, a full overhaul!

I did all this so I could get my life back. My house is a peaceful house now, not that we don't have our moments, but they are the exception not the norm. Last year, we went on an overnight hiking trip as a family. I cried most of the way because I knew that I had given my family these memories and they were hard earned.

Being a healthy person versus being an obese person is night and day. I always thought that if I avoided hard things, my life would be easier but the exact opposite was true. My life as an obese person was excruciatingly difficult and although getting healthy is the hardest thing I have ever done, my life is filled with love and joy.

In PHB progress is perfection and it took me a while for that to really sink in. It took me failing pretty hard a couple of times to realize that I could fail and still be a healthy person! In fact, each failure was a catalyst for my biggest breakthroughs.

Being able to deal with my failures has freed me from a miserable cycle of abuse and obesity, and allowed me to be in recovery from addiction.

Best part is, I have zero capacity left to feel like shit, physically or emotionally. I don't want to waste one more second back there. It serves no one and nothing. Life is for living and I am going to soak up every last drop.

———

Chrissy loves to travel and is always up for an adventure. In the 80's, she spent three years living in Hong Kong. Could this be where she mastered the ancient art of Karaoke? On wet Sundays you can find her out hiking; those rainy walks are her favourite. Chrissy couldn't imagine life without avocados, healthy fat is where it's at!

Chrissy McIntyre

projecthealthybody.com

ⓞ projecthealthychrissy

Margo

♥

First to Last

First pregnancy, first born…a beautiful baby girl. Her birth, the fulfillment of my lifelong desire to be a mom.

First sit up, first spit up, first sleep through the night, first solid food, first crawl leading to first steps, first words, first Mother's Day, first Christmas, and first birthday.

Marni, with her big blue eyes, is busy, quick-witted, creative, and full of life. Climbing trees and playing in forts, cutting her own hair…cutting her sister's hair, riding her bike, agilely scrambling over rocks along the rivers, chewing off the nose pieces of her glasses...over and over and over again, hiking boggy trails in the forest, playing hide and seek while exploring Alice Lake with her Grandad and then performing a "one-woman" show for him on the outdoor stage, skating lessons and dance classes, splashing at the pool.

Play-school and library programs readying her for school. So much to do and absorb. Witty and clever, learning is easy for Marni — following the rules and sitting still, not so much!

My inquisitive little girl lives life actively and engaged. With a mischievous grin, laughing easily at her own jokes and punny ways as well as anyone else's, Marni never misses an opportunity to live life with impulsive enthusiasm and abandon.

First day of high school, first heartache, first live theatre performance — in a real theatre with a real audience! First failed class, first Sea-Doo ride, first hospitalization, first choir trip — to Hawaii, first suspension, first honour roll. First time moving out.

Renting a cute one-bedroom flat in East Vancouver, Marni became an actor with Theatre For Living and was hired by Youth Co. as an HIV/Hep C peer support and education program worker. An avid advocate for the underdog, Marni was thriving in her work and theatre environments.

Throughout a child's life, there are so many antici-pated and expected firsts that are ooohhed and aaahhed over. As a parent we await these firsts and marvel as they happen. We think about what our chil-dren's futures may hold as we emotionally follow each step, agonizing over decisions made, behaviours cor-rected, discipline handed out, anger expressed and tears shed. Parenting takes us places we never expected, sometimes never wanted, and we are given lessons we did not know we needed to learn.

In a single moment, my world changes forever.

On May 2, 2020, a Police Officer walked up the drive-way. As he removes his hat, he says, "I'm sorry."

He continues talking but I no longer hear him. He doesn't need to say any more. I know. I understand… but I don't. I can't feel the ground beneath me and I go into the same pose I did while in labour with her: leaning up against a wall, burying my head in my arms, my legs crossed and my entire soul going deep, deep within while tears stream down my face.

The pain is excruciating. There is nothing anyone else can do to take it away. It requires all of my reserves to keep breathing. My head swirls as I think about our phone call the day before and our daily chats of the past week. She was full of spunk and had my guts hurting from laughter, she talked about setting up a special savings account and had plans to take her

Aunt out for a birthday Egg McMuffin. Our last phone call was so much fun.

Suddenly and unexpectedly, firsts become intrinsically entwined with lasts.

My last phone call with Marni, yesterday, means that today is the first day there won't be one – ever again. The following week is Mother's Day and it will be my first without her. How is that possible? Thank goodness our last Mother's Day was spent together, with her sister. Marni planned the day: Church in the morning, a joyful and chatty lunch at a small café followed by a sun-filled walk on the beach at Spanish Banks. What more could a mom ask for?!

Seven weeks to the day of her passing she would have turned twenty-nine. Last year, we celebrated her twenty-eighth birthday at our new home on Vancouver Island. I was giddy with excitement as I picked up Marni and her sister from the ferry for the weekend. I was always keen to have time with my kids and it was the first time these two would see the new place. We stopped in at Coombs Country Market to say hello to the 'Goats on the Roof,' and to nostalgically savour an ice cream cone before arriving at our home to enjoy dinner and a decadent chocolate birthday cake my partner had made.

Marni came home a handful of times during the first year we lived in our new community, her last visit two months prior to her death. She resisted leaving e.v.e.r.y.

time. On the morning of her last departure, I laid down on the bed next to her. I pestered her, sang silly good morning wake up songs, and took photos of the two of us while she rolled her eyes closed, with a slight grin on her face, and remained steadfastly snuggled under the cozy covers. We laughed and loved as though it was our last.

As Mama's, our children are always our babies and we never stop worrying about them. Despite our best efforts to keep them safe, life is not lived in a bubble and sometimes terrible accidents happen.

Last hug, last shared laugh, last text suggesting a new song to listen to, last dinner out, last live musical, last walk along the beach, last family photo, last goodbye at the ferry terminal, last provocative and insightful conversation about social justice issues, last trip to the Okanagan, last time hearing her voice. The list feels endless.

Life these days feels full of contradiction. Grief is tangled up in joy as my tears mix with laughter. My thoughts often go from light to dark and back again. It is oddly comforting to be going about my day and then, without warning, have tears fall as my heart remembers. Why is it we have words such as orphan and widow and yet there is no word for a parent whose child has died? Perhaps it is because the loss is truly both unfathomable and unspeakable.

Our first Christmas without Marni felt dull. Marni had always been the keeper of traditions with child-like wonder, excitement, and anticipation. No more 5:30 a.m. jumping on her sister's bed and exclaiming, "Wake up Hannah, it's CHRISTMAS!"

Tears quietly fell as we put up her Charlie Brown tree and hung ornaments she had made in kindergarten. Her sister made the candy cane cookies, I couldn't find the reason. They were Marni's favourite and she had baked them with me since she was three.

With a lifetime to come of firsts without Marni on earth, I am aware that I will have days that the best I can do is 'put one foot in front of the other,' and other days that will feel light and be filled with joy and laughter. Either way, as each day moves to the next, I am confident that the memories created with Marni will sustain me and the love will last.

———

Margo loves to unwind in the woods or by the water and enjoy a Diet Pepsi on the rocks. She's been a blessed "Patchwork mama" and foster parent to folks with diverse needs for thirty-two years. Margo holds a PhD in making people feel important and believes we are stronger together. Why order take out when your partner is a skilled foodie with a drawer full of ethnic spices ready to be deployed!

Margo Dent

dent_perspectives
Dent Perspectives

♥

Pep Talk:
Beautiful Begins Underneath.

I did a crazy thing after having babies. I threw out all my underwear.

The postpartum Walmart undies had to go. Now, commando may be your thing (you're cooler than me) but I'm a bikini brief kinda gal myself.

Underwear is like this strange time capsule of life. And do you really throw underwear out? Nope. You keep those neon green undies you bought at La Senza in college because why? The memories? Ha.

Your partner doesn't care what underwear you have on because he doesn't want you wearing underwear. And hear me on this, YOU are the sexy one. Not the underwear.

So go, dig out those undies. Open the draw and dump it out and say goodbye to the postpartum panties, neon thongs, too stretched, too small, ratty old undies.

Here's your permission slip to go buy new ones. All cotton, all comfortable, all body parts can be tucked in if necessary.

Life is like underwear. Change is good.

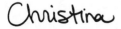

mara

♥

Rose and Thorn

My little fam jam of four loves traditions. My husband and I both bring some of these with us but the ones we've come up with on our own are so my favourite. For example we have a sheet cake in the freezer at all times in case of an emergency situation where someone is having an absolute garbage day. Also, exactly zero of us call each other our actual names — they call me the Captain. That's right, I'm not Mom to my family, they call me Captain. It's self-appointed but the name has stuck. I even have a key chain. My husband is Bobby because my daughter imposed b's instead of d's on a homemade Father's Day card when she was three and Daddy turned into a Bobby, again it stuck. My daughter (Kate) is Linda. Remember that very popular YouTube video "Listen to Me Linda" (google it), she's just as spirited. My son (Jack) is Larry, because it complimented Linda. Welcome to my perfectly imperfect family.

My absolute favourite tradition though has to be that twice a week, my sports-loving family and I make a point of talking about the best and worst parts of our day. We call it our rose and thorn.

Each time we do this, I watch my son and daughter as if I were watching a movie. What comes out of their mouths sometimes floors me. My kids are equal parts unforgettably clever and intensely honest. Often, they don't have a thorn in their day and moreover, the rose they recite was previously a thorn from another day that was solved organically or with a brainstormed strategy. As a team we have had some monster thorns that include the loss of a parent, a drawn out medical ordeal for our eldest child, and then the biggest thorn for me which has been navigating through an invisible illness.

I will never forget the moment a significant part of my life was stolen by vertigo and what was later diagnosed as Meniere's Disease, which is a balance and hearing disorder that mainly affects the inner ear and causes a cluster fuck to every part of your life (the last ten words are my contribution to the definition).

It was my son's first day of pre-school and I took the day off to be a cool mom who looked like she could always do drop off/pick up wearing a sick workout outfit as if I was about to go and kill it at the gym (aka go home and watch the Real Housewives with a hot cup of coffee). I picked up my three-year-old at the "end" of his two-hour day and we ventured to McDonald's to celebrate, then decided to eat at home and watch a show (don't worry it was Paw Patrol).

As I turned onto our street the world started spinning (think of being a kid and running in circles to make yourself dizzy). I have nightmares to this day thinking about how I pulled into our driveway subconsciously and thank every higher power for gifting me with some sort of auto pilot/blessing and we made it home safely. I called my husband who immediately left work and took me straight to the doctor, and then eventually to a specialist...and the years passed.

The years passed — it's been almost eight. I worked a corporate job, and had very understanding managers that didn't fire me when I would be out of commission for days, lying in bed and hoping the spinning would just stop. More importantly, I had my ride or die friends that would drive me home when the vertigo would embody me out of nowhere like a ghost to them, but an inevitable looming lightning strike for me.

One of the biggest blows is the side effect of losing my hearing. It's part of the disease that NO one can prepare you for. I have zero hearing capacity in my right ear and to make things extra spicy I live with a side effect called tinnitus which means hearing a fire alarm in my head ALL. OF. THE. TIME...and what makes it worse is no one can *see* that it's happening. The tinnitus has made me reclusive. I have become an extreme introvert who was previously the life of the party that no longer participates because she cannot hear it.

It's hard to admit that I'm not the same person I used to be. I'm not the fun loving woman my husband married. And while it kills me to think about it, he'll tell you he loves me more now, and I legit know he does. I don't feel bad saying this because he knows, but I thought Chris was kind of a dork when we met working at a restaurant. It wasn't until a failed staff outing that ended up just the two of us that I thought... hmmm...okay.

Chris is seven years older than me (which is a fun "how old was mom when you were_____?" game for your kids to play), and I find roses in each and every one of those extra years he has on me. He is filled with kindness, confidence, patience, support, perspective, tolerance, and just genuine love. And while I *do* know that I deserve these qualities, I pinch myself each moment I have them.

I was very recently asked what I could not live without and in a Late Night TV show speed round response I answered: My husband, and I legit mean it.

I've also gotten to watch my kids adapt to their Captain not feeling well — they make sure they're on my good side when we go for walks and they ask me if the TV is loud enough. They are my understanding little heroes...and maybe that's the best tiny rose somewhere in this giant thorn bush.

Honing in on the optimistic spirit of my kids I try to see the silver lining, and here is what I have discovered: while the effort to regain my affinity for social occasions, my health, and silly/fun self is exhausting and can feel slightly disingenuous (fake it until you make it), I've gradually learned that I don't have to be my illness. Instead I can choose to grow and be me in spite of it. I cannot escape what is going on inside my body. I can no longer be frustrated with others for not keeping my biggest thorn top of mind when it's something they can't see.

In situations that don't work well for my ailment I've learned to speak up and do the best I can. I get kudos for always being on time for meetings while what others don't know is that I have to be the first one there so I can find the seat that works best for my hearing. I've adapted to less sleep than one should ever have because sometimes the pitch of the fire alarm in my head adjusts and instead of waking up others in a panic (as I've done in the past), I just lie there. I've started going to noisy restaurants with my husband and we sit at the bar top so that I can be on his right hand side and we can have a conversation. I've become okay with not knowing what the conversation is about in social situations and also okay with asking people to repeat themselves.

Deep breath...and so, in the spirit of my kids with gorgeous rose coloured glasses (as they should be), and being better despite the things that have happened to me, today my thorn is that I'm freezing sitting in my car FAR too early in the morning on a "lazy Sunday," while my son has baseball practice, and my rose is that I get to be brave, put on my big girl pants, share this story with you, and that Jack and Kate will get to hear about it this evening at the dinner table (though I'll probably make up a less offensive thorn for Jack's sake)...and then maybe we'll eat a sheet cake.

―――――――

Mara's most cherished people are the ones she shares her home with. She LOVES to cook! Her favourite pastime is to sit with a cup of coffee in the morning reading a cookbook and planning a beautiful meal; her second favourite pastime is cooking it with a glass of wine. Peloton keeps her fit and healthy and questions like, 'do penguins have knees?' keep her up at night.

Tamara Blatz

Kieo

♥

The Power of Words

Feelings erupted as I hit the final kilometre coming back from a long trail run. Running a road that was familiar. With many unfamiliar feelings.

I wanted to scream. I was tense and confused. My body felt restless even as I ran. I was trying to make sense of how I got here.

My thoughts kept flashing back. I could hear the anger in his voice.

I felt the desperation. Why did this keep happening?

Don't call them stupid, those are our children.

The Run Against Stupid. I said it out loud. The words came out of my mouth in an audible epiphany.

I'd been running for years. Running was my time to reflect. On the trail my breath found its rhythm, this was my escape. I love people and I'm chatty but I cherish my time alone. I had made a habit of running in silence, using the time to pray and focus my mind on the person I wanted to be.

This run was the same but different. Circumstances were different.

The memories came like a movie reel. My daughter had handed me the keys, "The boys are in the truck already. Get us out of here."

She was only eight. The big sister to five younger brothers.

"He's mad, Mom, and he's in the garage. We've got to go now."

I took keys from her hand and we drove away.

My marriage was over. It was tearing me apart. My body was in agony. It ached so badly I had developed a painful autoimmune condition. I had not married who I'd imagined. I knew the truth in my heart from the beginning but young love can be blinding. We were kids when we met. I was only fifteen. You should have seen those deep brown eyes and the way they looked at me. I was captivated.

I was breaking from the grief of knowing I was never loved. Those eyes had lied. I was valued as a prized possession and not a cherished wife. We'd had six kids together. I knew our six precious children had lived through abuse, hurt, and pain. I'd married my hope and faith in the potential of a man who chose to hold on to his demons.

For so long I had prayed for an amazing outcome where I would be the saviour to a wild and immoral man. I wanted to witness his powerful transformation. I imagined us on the other side, him so thankful I had stood by him. I believed I would be praised for the love I had shown, my faith, forgiveness, and understanding. It was a beautiful fairy tale and I was the heroine. But it wasn't real. True love doesn't hurt.

The tears had drenched my neck warmer. He'd promised changes so many times. Why did it end this way? I had run forty kilometres in the freezing Ontario winter climate and the feelings erupting in my soul had me wanting to run a thousand more. My eyelashes were frozen together but running, the rhythm and the energy, were keeping me from crumbling

I kept running. Past my destination and on and on trying to figure it all out. I knew in my aching heart I couldn't ignore the damage caused by thoughtless words and angry hands. I knew this was a worldwide crisis that we needed to talk about. I wanted my children to know how valuable they were to me. I wanted to erase the awful words that had been spoken to them.

That cold winter day the Run Against Stupid was born.

We would run against the word stupid. An ugly word so many people use when they are angry or frustrated. I wanted to run against it and have it never spoken again! I knew that tempers escalate from angry words to violence.

When I finally returned from that trail run I sat with my children, shared my vision, and asked them to brainstorm and give their ideas for the run. That plan would become our summer adventure. We decided to run and explore together and use that time each day to encourage and build each other up.

As we shared our intention people got excited. The media wanted to share our story, a commercial was filmed, and a marketing team came together. The Run Against Stupid was going to change the world. It was all a go.

We'd planned it and were committed...until I wasn't.

I was overwhelmed by many conflicting emotions. For years I'd been taught to disappear, to not tell anyone my name, not want to be known, or heard. I didn't want to be misunderstood. I loved my family and still cared for my husband. I wasn't running against the man I had married, I was running to communicate that anyone who is repeating a destructive pattern could choose to learn from their past and the heartache caused.

The discussions with my kids lead us to recognize, "We are what we practice." It was time for people to intentionally practice kindness. Each day offers a new opportunity to be the person you want to be. It takes hard work and consistency. My kids and I had decided to intentionally practice.

That year we did The Run Against Stupid, for us. The timing wasn't right for publicity. That time would come.

We ran each day in a new city or town across Ontario. We ran, but more importantly we use that time outside to be thankful and positive. Our family of now seven travelled, camped, explored, and we ran. We talked, learned and grew. I could hear my kids being kind to one another. I was intentional about listening. We practiced how to express our feelings without being hurtful. Each day celebrating each other. What a blessing.

At eleven, nine, seven, five, three, and two they had very different abilities. Everyone was free to run, sometimes the little ones rode in the stroller, we ran laps on the track, we ran up and down the beach, we ran through the forest. We stayed together and helped each other. We hiked trails and biked to new places. We had fun, we laughed. The running turned into adventures. Lots of piggybacks. We would stop, explore, look at nature, and be intentional about enjoying the journey. We spend most of our time outside.

I am so thankful for that summer. Light and joy filled my soul. I was reclaiming myself. Each day I knew my children loved me and loved each other. I learned to be gentle with myself and forgiving of my mistakes. I learned to trust people, to care for and love my children. I learned that it was okay to have feelings and express them. I learned to be vulnerable. I validated my feelings when I hurt and as I flowed through that emotion. I allowed myself to embrace both the laughter and the tears. I put aside the expectation and judgement of society and found how to live my own values. A painful weight was lifting off my chest as I learned to be me again.

I believe one day our family project will become a global program that will spark change. That people all over the world will one day hear about our adventures and be motivated to go outside as a family with words of affirmation and encouragement. This was just the beginning.

This journey has been so hard. Being defined as a single mom has been uncomfortable. Raising six children is chaos. Even after all these efforts I still sometimes catch my kids using the word stupid and cringe. I'm doing my best and it's not perfect. My kids and I continue to enjoy our outdoor adventures together and I still cherish my runs alone.

Every time I lace up to head out the door for a run my kids come running to the door. "We need a hug, Mom." They each hold me tight and whisper, "I love you, Mommy." I'm captivated, but this time I know it's real.

———

Always on the move, Riece has travelled the world and loves exploring. She believes every day is a good day to be outside, especially in the rain! There is no such thing as bad weather, only inappropriate gear. Always open to new challenges, she started playing hockey this year and is the host of the empowering interview series "Reel with Riece." Her kids are her greatest joy.

Riece

reclaiming_a_dream

Emily

♥

Sober is My Superpower

Standing in the NICU looking at my day old son Nash, with a needle in his head and skin missing from his feet, was the most heartbreaking moment I've ever experienced. I was newly sober, in a new relationship, and now a new mom to a baby with special needs. What should have been one of the happiest times of my life, quickly became one of the saddest. If there was ever a time to say poor me, poor me, pour me a drink, this should have been it.

A team of doctors pulled my son's father and me into a family room, and said, "Please don't Google this, but we think your son has Epidermolysis Bullosa." The minute they left, we did what wasn't recommended. We saw images that are forever burned into my memory — tiny babies without skin on 50% of their bodies. I honestly thought that they were going to amputate his feet. Instead, I would learn that my first born child has a rare skin disease also known as EB which is often referred to as the worst disease you have never heard of. His body can't build the protein that holds his skin together. The slightest friction causes large blisters and skin shearing from head to toe — his skin as fragile as butterfly wings.

Nash would need to wear bandages up to his knees. At first glance, you'd never know he suffers from such an horrific disease. It's not until you remove the gauze dressings to see that his skin is raw and red almost down to the bone. The hardest part, there is no effective treatment or cure. How could this be happening to him — to us? For nine months I prayed every morning that we be given a healthy child. God did not deliver what I had asked for and man was I devastated.

In the past, I would have begged someone to sneak magnums of booze into the hospital to ease my excruciating pain. For seventeen years I drank and used cocaine through all emotions. Happy, sad, excited, nervous — I always needed something to make me feel right. I had never felt this type of agony before, but here I was S.O.B.E.R and Son Of a Bitch Everything was Real.

You see, I am an alcoholic and addict, who much like my son was born with painful diseases, mine are called alcoholism and addiction. These illnesses caused me to become a shell of a human being, someone who I hated for most of my lifetime. Growing up I never felt right — never good enough, smart enough, pretty enough, and certainly not skinny enough. Thing was I had it all — I took dance, played baseball, spent March breaks in Florida, and summers at the cottage. My parents never drank. They are hard working middle class people who gave me everything I ever wanted and needed.

For so many years, I could not understand why someone like me — a good person, who had a good life, consumed substances the way I did. I thought this only happened to people who had trauma in their lives. I now know that my childhood did not make me a drunk. A sickness that runs in my family did. Had I not found a program that taught me this and how to live clean and sober, I would not be alive today. For me, sobriety is a matter of life and death. It will either be a slow and painful alcoholic death or an overdose that will take my life within a matter of seconds.

Through doing a ton of work on myself, attending meetings, working with a sponsor, looking at my shit, and trying to clean up the wreckage of my past, the obsession to drink and use has been completely removed from me. I have not needed to be wasted in almost seven years.

Thankfully, I found a solution just in time. Two-and-a-half years before Nash was born, at the age of thirty, my life changed and I was graced with what I like to call my gift of sobriety. I was going to do so much in my second year alcohol and drug free. I was going to make up for the lost time in active addiction, but the universe had a different plan in store for me.

After five months of dating my son's father, I had a bun in the oven. Of course, I was scared and nervous — what new Mom isn't?! But I trusted that God had my back — that this pregnancy would be my reward for all the hard work I had done to get sober. Little did I know, labour would actually be the easy part.

After a few days in the hospital I learned that my son's first bath would not be in the kitchen sink. It would be a bleach bath in the NICU. Any infection that could be living in the open wounds on his little body must be killed. We would also need to learn how to do dressing changes and wound care — a regimen of hell that would need to be done at home, and continue until Nash could do it himself. I would lance blisters, remove dead skin from his wounds, administer narcotics for pain management, and wrap bandages around his feet. Something this postpartum mama was not mentally prepared for.

I had never imagined that my kitchen island and change pad would become a hospital bed. I did not think that my son's nursery would be filled with boxes of medical supplies — needles, scissors, creams, hundred dollar bandages that are used on burn victims. Some days I sob uncontrollably and drop countless F-bombs after accidentally poking my child with a needle or ripping the skin off his healing wounds.

Things got worse. Nash's father and I separated for the first time when he was six months old, and for good when he was two. Although I knew this was the right thing to do, I was absolutely gutted and would mourn the loss of the family I desperately wanted.

I was a single mom to a high needs child, working full time, while being a nurse morning and night. I cried myself to sleep. I ate my feelings and shopped myself through the depression, anger, and tears. I did everything in my power to keep showing up for Nash even on the saddest of days. However, you know what I did not do? I did not pick up a drink or a drug. I remained clean and sober through everything. Why? Because the alternative wasn't and still isn't an option for me. I will not let addiction take me from my child.

When Nash was fourteen months old, we were able to remove the bandages from his feet. A few weeks later he walked — something we thought he would never do.

Although his body is still covered in wounds and blisters, he rides a scooter, plays soccer, and has many friends who understand that Nashy has boo-boo's. My butterfly boy lives a fairly normal, very happy life. He has become my greatest teacher, molding me into the strong woman I was always meant to be. His determination and, "hold my juice box," attitude are infectious, ever reminding me that we're both lucky to be alive. Many with our diseases won't live to see their next birthday.

As for me — still sober, still single, still super tired, but so grateful to have weathered the storm with the help of a large village. I have the best group of girl-friends — many of them drink and I order a club soda on the rocks. These women carried me when I was weak. I have an honest, loving relationship with my family, and a job that I've been able to keep for almost eight years. Most importantly, I'm able to be a brave, present mama simply because I am sober.

Nash once said to me, "Mama, why do you always go to meetings?

"So I can be a good Mommy to you," I said.

He looked at me with sincere love in his eyes and said, "But you're already a good Mom."

The mother I am today is a direct result of doing the work to stay clean. Throughout my journey, I've always been told that if I want to keep what I have, I must give it away. So here I am, doing just that.

People often say to me, "I don't know how you do it?!"

I used to reply with, "I wasn't given a choice." But I was given a choice, and the tools to survive motherhood without getting loaded. I now know that sobriety is how I do it. Sober is my superpower.

———

Remarkably, Emily has sixty-one children — one biological and the sixty firefighters she looks after in her role as administrative assistant with Squamish Fire Rescue. She doesn't sing in the shower because she's usually talking to her four-year-old-son who is sitting on the toilet. Emily couldn't live without coffee, leggings, or the Big Book that saved her life.

Emily Tomlinson
emilyltomlinson

♥

Pep Talk:
What is Your Superpower?

We all have one.

Moms all have superhuman strength as we can do pretty much anything on three hours sleep including carrying seventeen bags of groceries in one load. We also have x–ray vision because we know the Kinder Surprise toy that is red (not the blue one) is under the couch next to the Happy Meal toy.

There may be times when your super hero skills feel they fail you and your Mama guilt creeps in. Trust your Mama instincts. Don't let that guilt be your kryptonite.

No one is YOU. **That is your superpower.** Knowing that can change everything. And remember, you look amazing in tights.

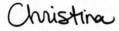

Ashley

♥

Mad Mommy

My daughter called me *Mad Mommy*. Again. I was filled with rage. I had the same dragon fire eyes that I had seen before, in my childhood. I learned at a young age that noise was unwelcomed. Crying, complaining, or high-pitched laughter was enough to get a flash of dragon eyes, and I was perpetuating this cycle.

I *was* a mad mommy. All of it made me mad. Cooking for the children and cleaning up after them. I was mad that I had to put on jackets and even more mad that I had to zip them up. My life felt so uncomfortable. Like those oversized–deli sausages at the supermarket, I was about to burst. I didn't have control over my anger. I thought if I only had a few more hours in the week or a bit more money, I could make my life and my schedule a bit more comfortable, and I would stop exploding so easily.

The routine had become mundane. Playing, chasing, feeding, cleaning, organizing activities, and preparing backpacks and snacks, but after all of that was done I found myself drowning. I was working evenings from my home office to make up for the items I didn't tick off the days or weeks before. I was frustrated that I couldn't do exactly what I wanted, when I wanted. I was emotionally exhausted; my performance at work was slipping, and I started having digestion issues.

I thrived on the organized chaos. When someone would tell me, "I don't know how you do it all," it would fuel me. Because it meant they could see how much I was doing and if I showed any signs of overwhelm or fatigue then I was weak, there was a crack in the system.

My fear and anxiety drove me to be more controlling. Controlling everything in my environment so I could anticipate what emotions I would have to deal with next. These were the coping tactics I was using to overshadow the internal shame I had been living with since my childhood.

I thought a midlife crisis meant driving a car that couldn't fit baby seats, wearing bejewelled jeans, and travelling the world while my kids were off on their own. But my kids were still in elementary school, I hadn't had my fortieth birthday bash in Vegas yet, and I was coming apart at the seams.

This was no longer a bad month, or a phase, like in my twenties when hair crimping and elastic belts made a short reappearance. I was being confronted from within and the uncertainty of my well–being was here to stay.

That summer we took a week-long road trip. Finally, a break. An extra set of hands to help as my husband is great at keeping the kids smiling and blanketing us with a sense of calm. I was a spectator when Daddy was around. I sat quietly on the beach while he got the kids ready for the water and I would be on standby when one of them needed comfort. If I could sense the day unstitching, it was permission to day-drink. I mean, it was vacation, the rule of five o'clock some-where was in full effect. The unfortunate thing about numbing fear and shame, is that I was also numbing happiness and joy.

My husband had a front row seat to the destruction, he had seen me frantically picking up the pieces in the months leading up to this trip. My birthday was coming up and one night around the campfire he asked, "Is next year going to look different?" He was done watching me spiral out of control. We have a beautiful partnership and I knew what he meant. He had the courage to say it to me. He had the courage to be kind to me and it was time for me to be kind to myself.

It took thirty-six trips around the sun for me to realize what I feared more than being a shitty mom was the fear of losing the closest people in my life. I took a booze break and I got started.

I called in the big dogs. The professionals. We all know what that means. There is no shame in talking to someone and having support outside your marriage, outside your family, or friendship circle. My therapist became another lifeline for me and like a scene from a divine film, I opened my arms, my chest, tilted my head back, eyes closed, heart open and said, "Just take me." I nourished myself from the inside out.

I dug into the dirty work. I reflected hard. I discovered that the burnout with work and life had awakened a cycle of shame that was deeply rooted in my parenting tactics. I revisited my childhood, reconnected with my inner child, and re-parented her. It was tough to remember "Little me," being unduly disciplined or receiving excessive punishment at a young age. The same age as my daughter. "Little me" needed more love, validation and safety. By re-parenting my inner child, I was immediately able to dial in my reactive parenting style. I started mothering like I wanted to.

I replayed all the major and minor events in my life that were taking up valuable real estate in my subconscious. I learned about connection, empathy and patience. I realized that fear and shame provided me with little time to open my schedule or my heart. I was told some harsh truths about reality. I was pretending I was fine. I was over-promising and under-delivering. I was meeting my children's struggles with impatience rather than empathy. I understood that over-responsibility is a trauma response. I empathized, knowing that people hurt you because they are trying to heal themselves. After a few months of bi-weekly therapy visits, I felt like I had just got off a carnival ride called *The Salad Spinner*.

I had figured out the parenting piece but my work was still a big trigger for me. I evaluated my worth based on the amount I was accomplishing, and this was easily fed because work always wanted more. One night I was sitting at the kitchen counter with my laptop and I dropped my head into my hands and cried. I knew I wasn't going to get anything done. I wiped my face, lifted my head, and told my husband I was releasing all of my clients, and we would figure it out along the way. It was that simple. I was done.

With my newfound freedom, I joined a book club. I got together with women on a weekly basis and found other ways to connect. I started answering my phone. I found less demanding clients and spoke positively, becoming fun to work with again. I answered the call that would be the solution to my immediate need for a new opportunity. I gained the confidence to reach for a business partnership. I started saying yes to invitations, claiming my free time in the mountains.

It turns out, a new car or twenty-something jeans doesn't even begin to measure up to the gift of claiming a more authentic version of yourself.

My life of adversity had provided courage for this inevitable awakening, and for the first time I am proud of myself. Initially it felt uncomfortable and I would blush when no one was looking. But now I am in love with the character I have built, the resilience I have stacked, and the mother I am transforming myself into.

There are always things to work on but my head and my heart are in tune and they have become more forgiving by embracing a bit of self-compassion. I am pleased to have my daughter talk back to me and roll her eyes. She isn't afraid of my reactions and no longer calls me Mad Mommy.

Like you, Ashley gets annoyed by people stopping in the middle of aisles or sidewalks as if they're the only ones in the world. She recharges with phone-off quiet moments and annual trips to Tofino. Ashley is a secret G who knows a surprising array of rap lyrics by heart and can be heard saying to her two little ones, "Yea, Let's do it!"

Ashley Hallinan

🄾 ashleyhallinan

Jessika

♥

Threads

Age 9 — Sexually abused by a family member for three years.

Age 14 — Raped at a party by a guy three years my senior.

Age 16 — Cheated on by my first serious boyfriend. The whole school found out which sent me into my first bout of depression.

Age 17 — Unplanned pregnancy. Devastating termination that took my soul with it.

Age 22 — Gave birth to my baby boy and quickly became a single mom working two jobs to support us.

Age 24 — After a devastating break up and being laid off from a job I had hoped would be my career, experienced my first serious 'meltdown.' Diagnosed officially with general anxiety disorder and depression.

Age 35 — Learned my husband of ten years was living a double life. Horrific, manipulating divorce that nearly broke me.

Age 37 — My otherwise healthy mom was diagnosed with stage four lung cancer and a mere six weeks later I held her hand as she passed away. More depression.

Age 38 — Working full time, running a business on the side, trying to get back to 'normal,' while not knowing what normal really was. Diagnosed with fibromyalgia. Burning out like a barely lit flame.

All my life, I felt like I was just hanging on by a thread. A delicate piece of thin string barely holding my complex life together. I was at my breaking point and knew I needed to make drastic changes. So, I quit my job, closed down my side business and headed off to Thailand, Singapore and Bali with my fifteen-year-old son. I was searching for who I was and I was searching for my next connection...the thread that would lead me where I was supposed to be in life.

I was reading the book the Alchemist, which is about looking for and following signs from the universe indicating you are on the right path. I was also taking stock of some potential career ideas. I had narrowed my options down to two ideas. Either opening up a store to sell vintage items, or using my passion for helping others, my coaching experience and my extensive life experiences to become a life coach. While waiting to get on the plane to Bali I looked up and noticed the man directly in front of me was reading the same book!

The Alchemist was not a new book so I found it odd that we were both getting on the same plane to Bali, my dream destination. The man had a beautiful welcoming smile so I held up my book and caught his attention. He jumped out of his seat, came over and gave me a solid high-five. I struck up a conversation with him, which was totally out of my wheelhouse. About thirty minutes later when it was time to board the plane, he shook my hand, introduced himself as Kevin Ross, and said goodbye.

Once I was in my seat, I googled his name and quickly discovered he was a life coach to life coaches!! He had written many books, had been on Oprah several times, and had had a private audience with the Dalai Lama. What an interesting connection and a possible thread!!

I quickly searched him up on Facebook and sent off a message explaining that we had just met in the airport and that I found it fascinating that he was in the line of work I was considering. I did NOT expect to hear back from him but I did invite him to have a coffee in Bali so we could chat about his career and see if it was something I should pursue. By the time our plane landed, there was a message in my inbox. I was so excited! Was it possible that this was the thread that might lead me to my next step in life?

Kevin invited my son and me to come to his six star resort for lunch and to spend the day with him. We had been backpacking and didn't have any nice clothes with us so when we arrived in our sink-washed, wrinkly, casual beach attire we certainly stood out...but he didn't care.

Over lunch, we had a wonderful conversation and then spent the afternoon having fun at the beach and pools. At the end of the day, he asked me, "What do you want from this?" I wasn't sure of what he meant. I started out by giving him all the reasons that he shouldn't help me: I have no job and no way of paying him, I live too far away, I'm not his level of client etc... The list was extensive but he just held his stance, continued to look me directly in the eye like nothing else was happening around us and waited. There was a long silence as I was trying to think about possibilities I didn't even know existed.

He asked me again, "What do you want from this?"

With all the courage I could gather, I blurted out, "I would love for you to become my coach and help me become a coach too."

That sentence would be the connecting thread that would propel my life forward.

Age 40 — Finished up my coaching with Kevin, completed my certification, and launched my life coaching business. I worked with a Youth Employment Program as well as coaching my own private clients and found my groove living my dream job. In the years after meeting Kevin I did a lot of work on myself and much necessary healing. I felt strong for the first time in years. I also felt called to go back to Bali to continue to heal, solo.

Age 41 — I boarded the plane to Bali for six weeks ALONE. This was my first time travelling on my own, and for that matter, the first time I did many things independently. In Bali I met many wonderful people, saw beautiful beaches and waterfalls, went to incredible temples, enjoyed playful monkeys, and even climbed a volcano in the middle of the night with a group of strangers. I was living my best life! I did sound healing, breathing exercises, and had some very powerful moments of release.

I will never forget the feeling of swinging high above the rice terraces on a huge swing. All that was holding me in place and preventing me from falling were two ropes of tightly woven threads, yet I felt completely free and safe.

Near the end of my trip I ended up joining twenty Brazilian women at a women's retreat. Again, completely out of my comfort zone, I enjoyed getting to know these women as we embarked on a healing adventure together. We did all kinds of exercises that allowed me to release much of the trauma and turmoil that still lingered in my body. It gave me the space to pull at the loose threads that were still present and see what would happen when I opened up those closed off portions of my life. It was a journey I will never forget.

When my time in Bali was over I called an Uber driver to take me to the airport and we had a great chat about my experiences while in Bali. As we pulled up to the airport he pulled three spools of thread out of a bag. He cut off a few strands of red, white and black thread and twisted them together. He tied the pieces of twisted threads on my wrist and told me to make a wish, explaining that the three colors represented my past, my future, and my current stage in life. He said that wearing it would remind me of where I have been, where I am now, and where I want to go next.

"When it breaks off your wish will come true," he said.

For eighteen months, I wore that bracelet next to the threaded bracelet from my mom's funeral. One arm adorned with bracelets from Tiffany & Co. and the other adorned with memories and connections. These threads...they are what hold us together. They are the moments we are not okay, the ending stages in life, and the beginnings. They remind us of what we have been through and where we are today. They are the past, they are the future, and they are the now.

Age 42 — I am no longer broken. I am a beautifully woven masterpiece of threads from all of my experiences. I am whole and I am strong.

Last week — The red, white and black bracelet tied to my wrist by a Balinese Uber driver fell to the ground. I am about to embark on a whole new chapter in my life, and I am ready.

———

Jessika grew up in a large family of carnival workers and started working at the early age of twelve. She is now an empty nester and a life coach working to restore women's inner sparkle through grace and self-love. Jessika loves to travel and enjoys blogging about her adventures including her latest adventure of living in her 'tiny home' called, 'My tiny gypsy rose'.

Jessika Houston

glitterngrace.com
🅾 glitterngracecoaching
🅕 Glitter and Grace Coaching
🅾 mytinygypsyrose

♥

Pep Talk:
You're a Unicorn!

Unicorns don't lose sleep over the opinions of little ponies.

Find your unicorns, don't waste your time in a field of horses. Be the unicorn because do you know what a herd of unicorns is called? A blessing. Ha! For real.

There is no need to fit in when you were born to sparkle, MomBabe! Because if you're going to rise, you might as well shine.

So dip today in glitter will ya! (Just don't spill it because no one wants to clean up glitter.)

Christina + Carolyn

Stephanie

♥

Permission

When my mum took her last breath, in some ways I felt like I took mine. And it's as if I've been holding onto that last breath ever since. No one asked me to pick up where she left off. No one asked me to take on her responsibilities. But I had an overwhelming sense of duty to do so to keep my family together. It felt like the baton had been passed to me and it was now my job to be the glue, the peacekeeper, the confidant, and the hostess. It was up to me to keep us going. To offer the stability and consistency she had provided so seemingly effortlessly. I had to take control, take ownership where she always did. Because if I didn't, who would?

I couldn't carry the burden of failure. Fearing the thought of her ever being disappointed in me. Afraid of not keeping my family as the strong and close unit it had proven to be. Or maybe I couldn't take the risk of potentially walking through grief in any other area of my life. Fearing how our family dynamic would change. Afraid of anyone seeing our imperfections. I was obligated to put on a brave face. Obligated to show up and move forward. Expected to pick up the pieces that had fallen to the ground. All while feeling unequipped to do so.

You see, she was phenomenal. Not perfect. But she did a lot of life really well. She made life look easy, like she had it all together. Even when that obviously wasn't true. She always worked full-time, but somehow managed to pick us up from school, put a meal on the table daily, and keep her house pristine. She rarely missed a sports event and used that time wisely connecting with other mums, even if they were from the opposite team. She was an incredible cook and enthusiastically took the opportunity to host dinner parties on the weekend. She loved red wine, bread, and chocolate and was known for dancing on tables.

It's easy to criticize where she failed. Communication in her marriage, lack of self-care or not living out her own dreams. But mostly she was a woman who knew exactly who she was. She was a five-foot-two firecracker with a height complex. She was known to wear four-inch wedges as slippers and use those same shoes to push a lawn mower across half an acre. She owned her story, never sat on the fence. She lit every room she entered with her bright smile and infectious laugh. She was opinionated, but rarely to her detriment. She believed that Christianity and kindness start at home. She had a wide range of friends and whatever insecurity she may have had, mostly around a lack of education, she made up for in her determination and drive. If you knew her, you loved her. She was a fighter.

My mum raised me to be strong and independent. She instilled in me morals and values that have made me the woman I am today. She taught me the significance of commitment. How critical it is to be honest. She taught me perseverance, and that my opinion matters. She taught me that nothing worthwhile is easy and hard work goes a long way. But most of all, she taught me that your word is all you have, and that people matter. She spent time being vulnerable with me, sharing stories of her life and the lessons she learned, in a way that made me feel like I was more than just her daughter, I was her friend. She respected me as a woman and yet always held me accountable.

I assumed that by being raised by the incredible, motherhood would come easily. Yet I quickly navigated feelings of inadequacy and feeling completely under qualified. It could be because the timing of her breast cancer journey so closely coincided with my path into motherhood. Managing the unknown in multiple areas of my life was overwhelming. All I could do was try to be brave and strong. To support her. But mostly not to burden her or add weight to her already heavy journey. I needed to echo her courage and exemplify the peace she portrayed.

As I laboured with my second child, my mother had her first seizure; the cancer had spread. This was the beginning of the end, the downward spiral into losing the woman I so greatly admired. The woman who, unknowingly, was my refuge.

It was never communicated. More a knighting I gave myself. To hold myself to the highest standards. To be strong and bold. To be vulnerable, but only when I have some control of the outcome. To prove myself in effort, because actions speak louder than words. All incredible attributes to have. However these became my assembled armour. Not quite knowing when or how to ask for help. Determined to persevere no matter how hard it felt, or how deep it hurt. I became disconnected. In my pursuit to disregard my devasta-tion, I ended up numb, almost desolate. I operated solely out of anger. In my effort to keep my mother's memory, her legacy alive, I ended up negating mine.

I so badly wanted to look like I was standing firmly in the chaos. I didn't give myself the permission to grieve, permission to process what we had walked through over the last few years. I was so desperately trying to put the pieces back together that I didn't notice I was falling apart. I had unknowingly enmeshed my own self confidence with the woman who loved me most. She had become my invisible compass, and without her I was lost.

I'm not exactly sure I'll ever feel whole again but for now I've given myself the permission to feel, to show up in my real emotions and to be seen, to sit in the uncomfortable, in the unrest, and embrace the hard. Knowing I'm not alone.

I was never meant to pick up where she left off. I am meant to learn from her mistakes, to challenge the adverse, and build on the beautiful. I don't need to only rely on her love but allow myself to find confidence in my own. To remind myself of who I am and who she raised me to be. I am worthy, regardless of the labels I wear. I am more than a mother, more than a daughter. I need to be authentic to who I am and to stand confidently in it. I'm not broken and I will be okay. In losing her, I have found more of her. But mostly more of myself.

A South African introverted extrovert, Stephanie's accent comes and goes depending on who she's talking to or how deep she is into the wine. A mom of three, people manager and husband's biggest fan, Stephanie loves watching people accomplish their dreams. She can't live without her toothbrush and regardless of the company can often be heard saying, "fuck."

Stephanie Atwell

satwell

Meg

♥

Creating the Life You Want

When I was a teenager, I would sneak out my bedroom window at night, smoke cigarettes, and listen to The Top 10 at 10:00 on AM radio while gazing at the stars. In my own world, singing along with the countdown, looking up at the sky in a smoky haze of dreaminess, I'd imagine that life would one day be better. It was my solo escape that brought focus, positivity, and hope to an otherwise chaotic upbringing.

I'm adopted. At fifteen days old, I went from a hospital in Saskatchewan, to join my adoptive family. My early childhood was filled with dance lessons, gymnastics, large extended family gatherings, and summer trips to my grandparent's cabin in upper New York State. This should have been the ideal way for adopted children to be brought up, but that idyllic family fell away.

My parents separated when I was nine and as my parent's marriage unraveled, so did my mother. She was grieving the end of her marriage, working as an elementary school teacher, managing a house, and solely caring for my brother and I; she began to fray.

I remember her becoming different, disconnected and overwhelmed. She was in the beginning phases of a substantial struggle with mental illness that had a profound impact on me. She tried so hard to keep things together, but frequently reached her breaking point. She would end up in the psychiatric ward of the hospital several times over the next eight years.

We went through an assortment of live-in nannies, coming and going as my mother did. I remember one nanny my brother and I would refer to as 'Mrs. D,' who's crisp apron was as stern as her demeanor.

I was commended for being a spirited yet mature and responsible child. I was expected to be the 'big girl,' to show the nannies how things worked and continue to be that compliant child who left behind her Barbies and My Little Pony to navigate an adult situation seemingly with ease.

In a world filled with uncertainty and expectation, I craved independence and autonomy. Not surprisingly I developed a strong aversion to rules, limits, constraints, and especially being told 'no.'

My bedroom was my sanctuary. Pearl Jam's Ten and Nirvana's Nevermind albums were staples, as was collecting magazines, cutting out pictures of objects, places, people and words I connected with. I intuitively stuck the cutouts onto the growing collage on my wall, creating a visual representation of what I'd imagined for my life. I had no idea how, when, or why, but I knew I wanted to create a new version of my life that unfolded beautifully, one that was well beyond the chaos of my current reality.

My mother was schizophrenic and when it got out of control she heard voices in her head. Each time she returned home from hospital, conflict arose because in her absence I had taken on the role of running the house. This power struggle was interpreted as my all-out rebellion.

I was sent to a group home for 'troubled teens.' A counsellor reaffirmed my deep belief that I wasn't a delinquent, rebellious teenager, but a by-product of so much uncertainty. Caught between two extremes: having the responsibility of an adult and then dramatically scaling back to assume the role of compliant child when my mom returned home. Throughout my time at the group home, I wrote. Every night I would sit at my desk, envisioning and expressing my knowing that there was something better.

At sixteen I moved into my very own apartment. A dreamy one-bedroom walk-up in an old heritage house in downtown Calgary, with a clawfoot soaker tub just like the picture I had on my wall. I didn't notice that this was the first piece of proof of some of the visions I had created coming to life.

I still spent time with my mother; she often called on me to drive her to the hospital when she was having an episode. We'd sit together for hours, holding hands, waiting for her to be whisked off to a room referred to by the inhabitants of the psych ward as 'The Fishbowl,' a glass room behind the nurses' station that was monitored 24/7. I would press the buzzer and hear the heavy click of the metal doors locking behind me each time I entered and left.

When I was eighteen my mother died in her sleep, two days before Christmas. She was forty-seven. She had been in the hospital days prior but begged to be released so she could spend her favourite holiday at home with her kids.

I immediately felt the need to shake up my life. The next summer I cooked for guests on horseback tours in the silent wilderness of Banff National Park. I moved to Maui for six months. I travelled around British Columbia throughout my twenties, first cooking for tree planters, then chasing wildfires while managing a catering company.

In an attempt to outrun the grief and the pain of the past, I thought that new experiences might fill the void I found in my life. I stopped visioning. I started to believe that I was broken and that life was beyond my control. I created a story that if things were going well, there had to be a karmic balancing and it was only a matter of time until the next tragedy fell into my life.

At the end of my twenties I became pregnant with my daughter, the brightest, loveliest invitation to re-connect to my innermost self. From the very beginning of my pregnancy she and I had a deep bond that grounded me in my quest to move through the grief. I didn't want to move into motherhood with a truckload of baggage so I committed to working on healing the losses in my life.

I learned that I felt limited when I held onto unhealthy patterns. I recognized that each time an old story came up, it was my job to poke holes in it. I learned the beauty in embracing grief and began to welcome the waves whenever they came, because each one brought with it a flow of beautiful memories of my mother. With each surge also came a piece of me that I keep collecting on my journey back to myself.

I again found myself cutting out images I was drawn to and posting them on the wall.

The new habit of questioning un-aligned beliefs and reconnecting with my visioning process helped me immensely during my next challenge: a five-year co-parenting dispute with close to fifty Provincial Court hearings, $120,000 in legal fees, and the complete depletion of my emotional energy as I navigated the court process while starting my first business.

I questioned the idea that I should thoroughly resent my daughter's father, that we would always have an adversarial relationship. I decided that those thoughts were simply not true. I could create a different outcome. I decided that someday we would have a positive co-parenting relationship because that would be healthiest for our daughter.

There were many moments where this vision seemed impossible, even laughable, but I held onto that hopeful belief.

I'm delighted to share that we've nurtured a friendly co-parenting experience. With the addition of my daughter's stepmother, who calmly walked into the eye of the storm with patience and grace. We now work together as a team in a way I'd always envisioned possible.

Though I don't smoke cigarettes anymore, I still frequently look up at the stars, listen to music, and create visions of my life to come. From building my own business, to solely owning a million-dollar home as a self-employed single mother, I've gained a tremendous amount of proof that my process of visioning and believing works.

———

Every morning it's lemon water, meditation, and journaling for Meg. She owns a decent set of power tools and used them to renovate her house. For Meg, sharing stories is the best way to better understand people...like the time she barrel raced and ran for high school Rodeo Queen decked out in tassels and gold sparkly things. It's unlikely you'll see Meg without hand lotion.

Meg Maclure

bungalow968.ca
🄾 megmaclure
🄾 bungalow968

♥

Acknowledgments

TO OUR FAMILY.

Our Mom, "The Doris."
This woman has sat on every sideline cheering for us since we were little girls. At every game, lesson or race, wherever we were, she was. Dad coached, Mom cheered. Dad may be cheering us on from heaven but Mom has a front row seat to the show. We would not be here without you. Thank you for your endless and unwavering support in allowing us to dream big and believing 110% we can do it.

Piper, Reece + Quinn.
Dream big little ones. Lead with passion, be brave, and remember you can do hard things. This will always be for you. We love you.

Our husbands, Peter + Brady.
You are our Stedmans. Thank you for allowing us to be Oprah. Love you.

TO THE WILD FEMME.

Jak + Rob.
Our business coaches turned friends who we asked, standing in a coffee shop with babies in our arms, "Is this even an idea?" And they said, "It can be anything you want it to be." Thank you for believing in us from day one.

TO OUR DREAM TEAM.

Anna, our speaking coach, you helped us see the field of dreams and led us to The Self Publishing Agency. You're a visionary. Megan, our publisher, you heard the whispers, followed them, and built a goddamn baseball field. Let's keep hitting home runs. Kristy, our designer, you knocked this one out of the park! Tara, our editor, you pitched the perfect game! Ira, our project manager, thank you for keeping score, you never dropped the ball!

TO THE MOMBABES.

To Our Authors - you can do anything, remember that. Thank you for believing in us and this book. You are all fearless. We love you.

Christina
+
Carolyn

We are sisters, and we can be yours too! It's actually a pretty good deal for you, we are here for hugs, pep talks, and we always share our fries.

Christina is older, but no one ever guesses that at first. She is the cook and Carolyn always says she can make something out of nothing. Carolyn is the baker and is up for any dessert request. She makes the best apple pumpkin hybrid pie. Thanksgiving is our favourite holiday.

Christina was voted 'rage against the system' in high-school and wonders if that's why she ended up in politics. Carolyn was class president in highschool now turned middle school teacher. Our roles are just an extension of believing in people and doing whatever we can to help people find and support their passions, goals, and big dreams.

Community is our philosophy, keeping it real is our jam.

Christina watches an episode of Seinfeld every night before bed, it was our Dad's favorite show and she used to fall asleep to roaring laughter from downstairs. Carolyn stays up late watching home decor shows and perusing real estate websites so she can one day build a dream family farm for us all to live together.

We are moms to three babes: Christina has two girls and Carolyn has a little boy. We live in the suburbs outside Vancouver and only Carolyn drives a minivan. You will always find us with a coffee in hand, humming Dolly Parton, and trying to read the next best seller without falling asleep.

themombabes.com
🖸 themombabes
photo cred: Grinning Weasel Photography